ILLUSTRATED HANDBOOK OF
WESTERN EUROPEAN
COSTUME

THIRTEENTH TO MID-NINETEENTH CENTURY

TWO VOLUMES BOUND AS ONE

VOLUME ONE: THIRTEENTH TO SEVENTEENTH CENTURY

IRIS BROOKE

DOVER PUBLICATIONS, INC.
Mineola, New York

Bibliographical Note

This Dover edition, first published in 2003, is an unabridged republication of the following two volumes bound as one: *Western European Costume: Thirteenth to Seventeenth Century, And Its Relation to the Theatre* (Volume One) and *Western European Costume: Seventeenth to Mid-Nineteenth Century, And Its Relation to the Theatre* (Volume Two) originally published in 1939 and 1940, respectively, by George G. Harrap & Co. Ltd., London. The only significant alteration consists in moving all thirty-two color plates (from both volumes) into a full-color insert after page 144 of Volume One.

Library of Congress Cataloging-in-Publication Data

Brooke, Iris.
　　[Western European costume . . . and its relation to the theatre]
　　Illustrated handbook of Western European costume, thirteenth to mid-nineteenth century / Iris Brooke.
　　　　p. cm.
　　"Two volumes bound as one."
　　"An unabridged republication of the following two volumes bound as one: Western European costume, thirteenth to seventeenth century, and its relation to the theatre (volume one) and Western European costume, seventeenth to mid-nineteenth century, and its relation to the theatre (volume two), originally published in 1939 and 1940 respectively by George G. Harrap & Co., Ltd., London" — Verso t.p.
　　Includes index.
　　ISBN 0-486-42747-1 (pbk.)
　　1. Costume — Europe — History. I. Title.

GT270.B73 2003
391'.0094 — dc21

2002041669

Manufactured in the United States of America
Dover Publications, Inc., 31 East 2nd Street, Mineola, N.Y. 11501

ILLUSTRATIONS

PLATES IN COLOUR*

ILLUSTRATIONS IN THE TEXT

*For this edition, all the color plates are bound together between pages 144 and 145 of Volume One. Their original page positions appear above.

INTRODUCTION

IN view of the highly finished productions of period plays and adaptations from the old masters of dramatic art to be seen in the theatre of to-day, it seems hardly credible that a little over a century and a half ago the production of any play, however ancient its origin, was performed in the contemporary habits of the actors and actresses—little or no attempt being made to reproduce the author's original vision of his work.

With the advancement of interest in so-called 'Period plays' and films of historical interest, a wider knowledge is perhaps desirable of how any playwright or author originally saw his characters clothed.

The purpose of this book, then, is to give some of the more unusual styles and fashions worn since the theatre commenced to be a leading interest in Western Europe, and also to give the names of several authors whose work may possibly be utilized for theatrical purposes again.

That the early dramatists wrote much that has not been used on the stage or screen is an undoubted fact, and many themes for very attractive productions are still to be found in the plots of the old Italian, Spanish, and very early French authors.

The northern European countries were probably too concerned with the religious aspect of the theatre to adventure far into the fields of romance and fantasy, and it was not until the end of the sixteenth century that the secular stage was an established feature in Germany and Holland.

A rather difficult problem arises here concerning the

simplest means of classing the various countries or dukedoms that went to the eventual composition of Germany as we know it to-day.

As this book does not pretend to give an historical and geographical record, it will perhaps be easier to follow if they are collectively alluded to as 'Germany.' Strictly speaking, the term is rather wide of the mark, because each and every division had its own particular style and fashion, and it would be almost an impossible task to sort and name them all. I must, therefore, plead the excuse that their relativity to the theatre is practically negligible.

For those who are not consulting this book in a theatrical light, but merely from the point of view of con-trasting styles in European clothing, there are sufficient examples in the ensuing pages to give quite a comprehen-sive knowledge of the various differences in cut and style without plunging into the intricacies of the history and geography of Germany.

It must be borne in mind that, although at certain times the clothes worn in two different countries at correspond-ing dates are strangely different, it is quite probable that they might have been both worn in the same town at the same time.

People travelled a great deal, in spite of the dangers and difficulties they had to face. And in many records of the period one finds allusion to the strangeness of a foreigner's clothing, and how certain travellers were forced to adopt the clothes of the country in which they were travelling so that they did not advertise their nationality.

The fifteenth and sixteenth centuries seem to have most striking differences in national styles, or this may possibly be more obvious because of the scarcity of existing examples of the earlier centuries. It is nevertheless a curious fact that countries so far apart as Spain and North Germany happened to be wearing almost identical styles at identical dates during the thirteenth and fourteenth centuries. To whom goes the credit of their original inspiration ?

The fourteenth century gives even more food for thought in this respect, because the styles were not, strictly speaking, entirely practical and obvious as were those of the thirteenth and earlier. The cut-away cote-hardies and surcoats of the fourteenth-century ladies were universally worn, and they certainly appear to our modern eyes as a mere freak of fashion, for they served no particularly useful purpose. The same might be said of other eccentricities of the century—long-tongued sleeves, tippets, the pocket-like slits in the gowns, the curious liripipe and hood, and numerous other peculiarities.

Many of the differences in styles may be put down to the different types of materials spun and woven in each country.

That the warmer countries were privileged in this essential may have had a lot to do with so many styles being of Spanish and Italian origin. Both sheep and silkworms can flourish in a warm and temperate climate. The northern countries were either forced to pay colossal sums for their imported silks or else to clothe themselves in wool and cotton—thus we see so many of the German and Dutch styles in heavy materials enlivened with linen collars and other extras. At the same time, France is privileged to adopt both styles, and Italy and Spain luxuriate in a wealth of brilliant shimmering silks.

The colours, too, were affected by the fabrics on which they were applied. And as the art of dyeing had not advanced to quite the remarkable range which we have at our disposal to-day—the silk and cotton fabrics only would take the pastel shades. Wool—being of a brownish grey when natural—must always have slightly dulled the brilliance of the finished article.

A point of great value to the would-be producer of plays of this period is that, as there was no imitation silk with its crude brilliance, the mat surface of silks was neither attempted nor attained—silks of the Middle Ages and sixteenth century glistened with a lustrous sheen—the higher the reflective values the better the silk, and many clever effects can be arranged with the assistance of a brilliantly shining material in conjunction with a heavier, more sombre, fabric.

THIRTEENTH CENTURY

THE aim and scope of this book is to point out differences in costumes, and the manner in which those costumes were worn at corresponding dates, in the more important countries of Western Europe—France, Germany, Italy, Spain, Denmark, and the Netherlands—also to give their connexions in relation to the theatre and dramatists contemporary with them, in the hope that any one wishing to obtain information regarding a dramatist's work at a certain period may be able, with the least possible research, to ascertain the principles governing the methods of dress at that particular date.

Several difficulties arise to harass and obscure the student's views on this subject. Possibly the most trying is to separate the peculiar persistence of buffoonery and masked slap-stick comedy from the themes of traditional drama. A Comic Theatre existed and flourished as early as the fourteenth century, and in the sixteenth century the now familiar figures of Pantaloon, Harlequin, and Punchinnello, derived perhaps from the old Roman Theatre, make their appearance in every country in Europe. The last remnant of these eccentricities are still to be found in our Christmas Pantomimes of to-day. Their fantastic human animals, clowns, columbines and harlequins, and boisterous, childish buffoonery—in conjunction with a time-worn but pretty theme to please more sugary sentiments—owe their origin to the Profane Theatre of the Middle Ages and the Jugglers' and Fools' Fair of earlier days.

Secular drama of the Middle Ages abounded in theatrical

disguises—false heads, fools' caps, masks, patchwork coats (harlequin again), and a sort of pseudo-Greek armorial effect—the latter reserved for the most part for the more religious aspects of the production. It is almost impossible to separate the Secular from the Religious—as far back as the thirteenth century. So many plays or mimes were written as an expression of satirical gibe—and a moralistic attitude towards the sins of the flesh—that a heavy religious flavour might creep into a peculiarly obscene text. The reflection on costume with these semi-religious plays is too intricate to attempt to deal with, and we therefore must content ourselves with the more straightforward productions and those written in the style of Revues or Comic Opera.

As this book is to deal with contemporaneous clothes and their relation to the theatre, there is little worthy of note prior to the institution of the Profane Theatre—during the second half of the thirteenth century. Earlier than this the theatre in Europe was regarded purely as a means of making Biblical scenes more realistic. Miracle plays were perhaps the earliest method of religious instructions commenced at a date when almost the only educated people were to be found in the Church.

There were, of course, the travelling Troubadours, ' Jongleurs,' acrobats, animal imitators, and those who travelled with performing bears and horses, and the ' torna-trices '—female tumblers. Old manuscripts are rich with illustrations of those then-called ' Obscenities,' but no worthy record indicates that anything approaching secular farce existed until about 1260.

The religious fervour with which the theatre has been attacked so drastically from time to time was still obvious as recently as the last century. This attitude is distinctly

Fig. 1

traceable to the theatre's original and fundamental Pagan inspiration. While the Church held the stage as a means for the propagation of Miracle Plays, the production of non-religious plays—inspired by the Ancient Greeks and Romans—was obviously to be condemned as being in direct competition to the contemporary religious views which sought to bind Christendom in ecclesiastical fetters.

The modes and manners of each century in European history are directly traceable to a leading culture in one particular country.

The cult of the thirteenth century was, then, influenced by the definitely advanced standard of living in France under Louis IX (called Saint Louis); and, to help us here, we have the valuable records of Jean de Joinville, who was Louis's personal friend for many years. Joinville shows us three outstanding facts in relation to clothes worn in mid-thirteenth-century France. First, that the really good garments lasted undated for many decades—the king queries if he, Joinville, is not embarrassed by being better dressed than the king himself. Joinville replies, " The dress I wear, such as you see it, was left me by my ancestors—I have not had it made from my own authority." From this also we may learn that any attempt at strict dating of certain garments is obviously out of the question. ' My ancestors' might mean fifty years or even more.

Second, a great deal more importance was attached to the refinements of dress and its impression on the fair sex than one might expect at such an early date. " Every one ought to dress himself decently in order to be more beloved by his wife and more esteemed by his dependents. The wise man says we ought to dress ourselves in such manner that the more observing part of mankind may

Fig. 2

not think we clothe ourselves too grandly—nor the younger part say we dress too plainly." Here is a worthy and thoughtful sentiment adequately expressed.

Thirdly, King Louis IX dressed both neatly and well himself, thus establishing a shining example in fastidiousness to an eager and imitative populace—who had previously been taught that good clothes were sinful and selfish.

Of this Joinville writes :

" . . . Often have I seen him come into the Paris gardens dressed in a camlet coat, with an overcoat of woollen stuff (without sleeves), a cloak of black taffetas fastened round his neck. Neatly combed, having no cap (coif) but merely a hat with white peacock's feathers on his head."

Another item of valuable data to us is that this king —though religious to a degree—did *not* condemn the jongleurs, acrobats, and travelling troubadours as the Church did. For although the Church held that no actor could expect anything but hell in the after-life, and must therefore be persecuted in this one, the king encouraged them so far as to exempt them from all tolls and taxes, making them pay for these things in their own manner— *i.e.* to recite, sing, or dance at the toll gates or bridges to amuse the guards.

Under this kindly attitude there flourished the first purely secular playwright—Adam de la Halle, or Adam Le Bossu. Born in Arras about 1235, he studied at the University of Paris during the lifetime of this illustrious king. His first dramatic work was executed while he was still at the university—this was *Le Jeu de la Feuillée*, a satirical comedy entirely free from religious inspiration.

His work is admirable in his ability to strike a happy

Fig. 3

note in his excellent combination of satirical review, operetta, and dramatic pastoral.

His most noteworthy work, however, was done in 1282, when he devised *Le Jeu de Robin et de Marion*. This playlet he wrote while in Naples to amuse the Neapolitan Court —quite probably it has a direct connexion with our all-familiar story of Robin Hood and Maid Marian—though the theme is hardly compatible. In this delightful satire we have the oldest comic opera extant.

Another French playwright who lived during the thirteenth century was Jean Bodel of Arras—who was of the same school as Adam, though a few years earlier. In consequence, his works smack strongly of religion. His most noteworthy work, *Le Jeu de St Nicolas*, despite its title, might be classed with the Profane Theatre, but although the scenes enacted include those of familiar life in tavern and brothel they are freely flavoured by extracts from the Gospels, and the whole finishes with the *Te Deum*.

By the close of the thirteenth century, Secular Drama had its place as an entirely separate art from the Religious Drama, though the latter continued to hold its own well into the sixteenth century. But ecclesiastical fetters had failed irretrievably to bind the stage to the Church.

That the contemporary clothes of the thirteenth century were curiously unsuitable for any vigorous or speedy movement is perhaps the first most noticeable factor in relation to clothes and the stage. Thus we find that the young girl in Miracle plays frequently abandons her hood, head-dress, and veil, and appears with flowing locks and shortened kirtle. Here, then, is something over which the Church might see fit to raise a storm of abuse and indignant protest. The good woman of the thirteenth century was

Fig. 4

still much hampered by the bigoted preachings of St Paul. Violent religious protests had been levelled at the tight-lacing and uncovered heads of the mid-twelfth century, and the re-adoption of veiled heads and loose-fitting gowns (Fig. 1) that disguised feminine attraction quite possibly led the Church to assume that their protests had been heeded! In all probability this had nothing to do with the changes of fashion—but nevertheless the secular stage was obviously regarded as a dangerous enemy to conventional modesties.

The crespin, barbette, and fillet (hair net, chin band, and fluted or goffered head-band) formed the traditional head-dress of the century (Fig. 2). All or one of these could be worn in conjunction with a head-veil and wimple which covered the neck and throat. The gown was loose-fitting and worn over a kirtle of contrasting colour—the voluminous folds of the gown held in place at the waist by an ornamental girdle or belt; its richness signifying the quality of its wearer. Over this was worn a circular cloak fastened at the throat with a brooch or tied with a cord and an ornamental button on each side of the throat.

In France the *garde-corps* was worn in place of the cloak. It (Fig. 3) was a complicated but dignified garment with full hanging sleeves, with a slit for the arm at elbow height, and a hood that could either be worn as a collar or drawn over the head in cold weather. This garment was worn by both men and women, the only difference being that the feminine version was usually more voluminous, and touched the ground all round.

In France also more licence seems to have been allowed in the manner of shaping garments and hairdressing—as will be seen in Fig. 5. Neither of these gowns follow closely on the more traditional dress of Figs. 2 and 4.

France and Italy were perhaps more advanced in

Fig. 5

their fashions. The northern countries were more inclined to volume than elegance and individuality. Italy specialized in exquisite embroidered borders. The lines of their gowns followed the classical styles very closely, even to the split sleeve and shoulder clasped together at equal intervals. The gowns were very long, but were more often than not gathered up into one or more bands to facilitate movement (Fig. 6).

The men's clothes, too, were simple and extremely practical. The tunica, or tunic, was worn over another similar in cut, but usually longer and with tight-fitting sleeves. The skirts were 'gored' at frequent intervals so that they hung from the waist in a series of fluted folds. The fashion for dragging them tightly across the stomach so that V-shaped folds appeared in front and a heavy, swinging bunch of fullness at each side was still to be seen until the close of the thirteenth century.

Fig. 6

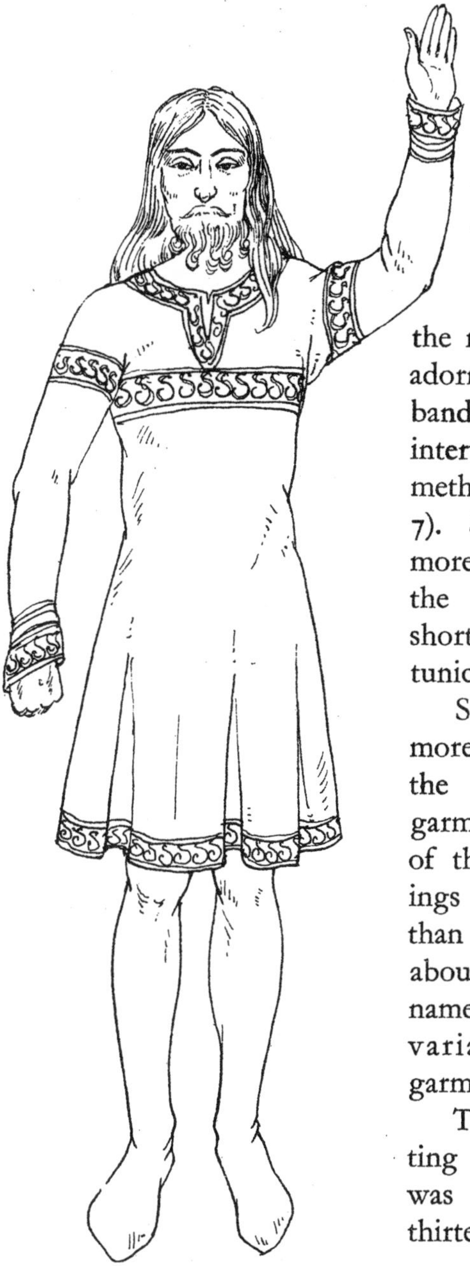

The longer, more sedate gowns or tunics were not figure-fitting, but were fastened at the waist with a leather girdle or jewelled metal belt.

The use of jewels and semi-precious stones was the most popular method of adorning a robe—strips and bands of embroideries at equal intervals were also a popular method of decoration (Fig. 7). Small spot-patterns were more often employed for the adornment of the shorter, more serviceable, tunic.

Since we are concerned more with effect than the intricacies of under-garments, etc., a careful study of the accompanying drawings is of far more value than a detailed description abounding in contemporary names for the numerous variations of certain garments.

That the fashion for cutting materials on the cross was persistent during the thirteenth century must be

Fig. 7

remembered—the draped neckline, V-shaped sleeves, and circular skirts cannot be fairly imitated if cut on the straight of the material.

Hairdressing and beards, too, merit that special import-ance should be attached to them. The thirteenth-century man wore his hair dressed with an elaboration of style almost amounting to the curled and set fashions worn by the women of to-day. The usual length of hair was between the nape of the neck and the shoulders—the ends were curled, either in a series of clustering ringlets or turned in or out in one scroll of curls. The front hair was cut shorter, forming a curled fringe framing the face. The employment of coifs or bonnet-like caps to hold the well-groomed hair in place gave the men a ludicrous effect of being disguised as babies.

Such refinements as leather gloves and tight-fitting leather shoes, encrusted with jewels and often covered with gold mesh, signified the quality of the wearer. For the most part, the gentlemen of quality favoured the longer and more dignified garments—these could be tucked up into the belt when more freedom for the legs was required —such as when hunting, hawking, etc. When this was the case, the hose and their attachment to the braies, or drawers, were clearly visible, as also were the somewhat clumsy braies or trousers tucked up and resembling a species of linen plus-fours (Fig. 8). The hose rarely reached higher than mid-thigh, and the tops might be ornamented with embroideries. The peculiar passion for horizontal stripings was frequently exemplified even in this item of apparel.

In some cases the hose were pinned to the linen braies with large ornamental brooches; at other times, when perhaps they were longer, they were tied to the under-belt

Fig. 8

at the waist with strings. Occasionally, when the short hose of an earlier date were worn, they barely covered the knee and were held in place by the knotted ends of the braies.

With regard to general methods and styles in ornaments, metal and gems played a very important part. The almost staggering weight of the richly adorned garments must have been a great trial to any one engaged in any active pursuits. It is therefore feasible to believe that the richly ornamented gowns and tunics were reserved for state functions and purely formal wear.

Gems were fitted into the weave of the cloth and made pattern both at the throat and hem. Some method must have been devised so that their weight did not tear the materials to pieces, but exactly what it was it is impossible to surmise. Some of the gems were set in gold mesh-work, or even in some cases appear to have almost a solid foundation of gold or silver. In representations of this we can see clearly a squareness in the fitting of the collar, and the bands at the bottom of the tunic have a hinged effect.

Simple motifs were employed for the design on such garments—fleur-de-lis, diamonds, ovals, crosses, trefoils, and a numerous variety of geometric designs being the most frequently employed. Sometimes, however, on the very large surfaces of cloaks one may find the more simple device of a repeating all-over pattern; the theme of these was usually based on a curved and curled brush stroke. Otherwise, an heraldic simplicity governed all forms of design, the already-mentioned inclination to horizontal stripings frequently being the foundation for numerous motif designs, enclosed within the stripes.

The heavy ornamentation of scabbards, belts, shoes, and gloves of state was essentially a prerogative of the

Fig. 9

wealthy lords and kings. Swords were not worn with civil attire as, at this early date, they were too massive and encrusted with precious stones and jewels to be lightly carried about. It was one of the esquire's privileges to stagger beneath the weight of his lord's sword. The ceremony of girding on the sword and belt before battle was quite a traditional scene.

It is, however, a frequent fault perpetrated by the theatre to represent a knight in civil attire complete with sword and scabbard. The fashion for wearing the sword as an extravagant piece of everyday attire was not indulged until the sixteenth century.

The only accessories of jewellery worn during the thirteenth century were rings and brooches and an occasional wide, gem-studded pair of bracelets. Necklaces and ear-rings were conspicuous by their absence.

Buttons made their appearance in a serviceable capacity towards the close of the thirteenth century—and their attractions as a means of ornament very quickly superseded their popularity from a purely utilitarian point of view. They were employed not singly but in rows of eight or a dozen, from wrist to elbow and down the front of the *garde-corps*.

The flared simplicity of the waistless, ungirdled gowns worn by the women at the end of the thirteenth century seems to have been adopted only by those of high rank. Probably the voluminous unrestrained folds, though dignified and very effective in their sweeping lines, were a little unpractical for the woman who must busy herself among her household duties (Fig. 9). For grace and effect they relied entirely on their cut. No ornamentation or bands of embroidery broke their dignified simplicity. They were probably made of the richest materials, and a single brooch or plaque at the throat was the only ornament allowed. The great cloaks worn at this time were usually lined with fur and cut in a complete half circle, the fur lining frequently showing at the throat and forming a sort of collar.

Hats, head-dresses, and shoes are items of the utmost importance and change with a more frequent rapidity than the larger and more expensive garments.

The shoes of the early Middle Ages were varied and amazingly interesting in their complexities of shapes and designs. They were made from a very flexible leather and gave the foot an appearance of being clad only in a stocking. Numerous examples have been included in the accompanying drawings, but there seems to be an almost inexhaustible variety of designs in them in contemporary drawings. The more usual shape, perhaps, was that which was slit up the instep and fastened at the ankle in front with one bead or button. Shoes were usually decorated in some way either with jewels or embroidered 'cuffs.' A more serviceable type, perhaps, was that which reached well over the ankle and was secured on one side by a short strap pulled through a ring, probably the ancestor of the buckled shoe.

Women's shoes were similar, but the 'cuffed' ones and those that came over the ankle were only worn by the men. During the last few years of the century the elongation of the toe became a fashionable feature—an absurdity to be exaggerated and rendered ridiculous during the subsequent century.

For domestic wear the hose were often soled with leather (Fig. 10), rendering a shoe unnecessary ; and in more rural districts the peasants frequently went unshod, merely binding their ankles to save them from the more violent attacks from nettles and brambles, their feet being

hardened by exposure to a greater
degree of resistance than their legs.

As has already been mentioned, the
coif was a generally accepted form of
head-dress, and its decoration an object
of great moment. Bands of contrasting
materials, embroidered motifs, and a
shaping accentuated by geometric
designs, obviously proved
an amusing occupation for
the needles of the wives,
mothers, and sisters of the
wearers. Besides the coif,
the hood was also of primary
importance. During the earlier
part of the century the hood had
been part and parcel of the
cloak or mantle worn outdoors,
but by about 1250 it had become
a separate garment, covering the
head and shoulders, and with a
small point at the top. Before
the close of the century the
point had become the chief
feature of the garment and had
been enlarged upon and elongated
until it assumed the proportion
of a tube two or three feet long.

The rather clever shaping of
the hood at this time will be
noticed in the accompanying
drawings taken from photographs of an actual hood

Fig. 10

found in Greenland in recent years (Fig. 11). The seam, being cut on the cross, shapes to the neck so that a minimum of bulk with a maximum of freedom are excellently blended characteristics. The shoulders also cling closely to the form without unnecessary crease or bulge. The

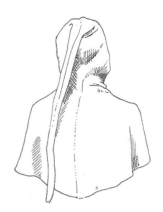

Fig. 11

traditional idea of the hood's simplicity and lack of shaping is for ever exploded on contemplation of these unique original garments unearthed in perfect condition after an interment of nearly six hundred years.[1]

The inclination towards points, first noticeable prob-ably in the re-adoption of the Phrygian cap of the eleventh century, with its punch-like hooded peak, became more

[1] *Viking Settlers in Greenland.* (Cambridge University Press.)

and more marked during the thirteenth century, and during the second half of the century became the main inspiration for all forms of head-dress—with the one exception of the coif (Fig. 12). All the caps and hats finished with a point or tuft on top, and as they for the most part lacked any brim it is quite feasible to surmise that these appendages were supplied as a sort of handle with which to raise the hat. Whether or not the point was put to practical use is, of course, a trivial detail; but nevertheless the fashion persisted for some fifty years, and the most peculiar effects were the result. Points, tufts, knobs, and hooks ornamented the centre of the little striped caps, and in combination with the long sweeping styles of formal dress had a ludicrous effect.

With women, head-dress and hairdressing—the intricate variety of ways in which the crespin, barbette, wimple, and fillet might be worn—served to amuse the thirteenth-century ladies for several generations.

The crespin could be merely a linen bag in which the hair was bundled and pushed conveniently out of the way, or it might be quite a complicated network of gold mesh set with gems and precious stones wherein the hair was neatly arranged in heavy, rolled plaits. The shape of the crespin of necessity followed the line of the hair-dressing beneath. Sometimes this was done in a single low chignon hanging to the shoulders at the back, or divided into separate plaits rolled and worn low upon the neck. Or again it might be filled out with the hair arranged high up in plaits or rolls over the ears, leaving the neck bare.

There were also occasions when the crespin was entirely dispensed with and the hair worn loose beneath the barbette, though probably this was done only for

Fig. 12

more decorative occasions, as the very long flowing locks must have been a great trial to a woman when she was engaged in domestic pursuits.

The barbette varied in width from two inches to about six inches, the wider ones being more often of transparent fineness. Often it was worn draped under the chin and fixed to the plaits over the ears with pins, but more often it completely encircled the face and was fastened at one side, or on top of the head. Occasionally the effect of barbette and fillet was obtained by a long piece of material wound round the chin, over the head, caught at the side, and then wound round the head, fastening at the point it started from.

The fillet was obviously derived from the fashion of wearing coronets and circlets. It varied considerably in width and slanted outward slightly towards the top. The earlier editions were circular and simple—the hair being worn rather low on the neck, but by the middle of the century they were goffered, frilled, and scalloped, and the circular shape had become an oval so that it might fit better over the hair when worn in shells over the ears. Sometimes these fillets appear to be worn with a little skullcap underneath, and from this fashion another evolved in the introduction of a flat top for the fillet, transforming it into a little pill-box hat.

Little attempt has been made in this chapter to show the differences in Continental fashions.

That France was the leader of fashion during the early Middle Ages is an indisputable fact; there are numerous references in thirteenth-century manuscripts that allude to Paris fashions.

The Italians were perhaps the most advanced in their methods of fabric decoration, and a form of wood-block printing existed as early as the beginning of the century. Their designs still held much of the earlier traditional features of the old Roman Empire.

From Spain, Sicily, and Venice came the finest and fairest silks—the northern countries being more expert in the manufacture of woollens and fustians (a mixture of wool and linen). But apart from these refinements the general shaping of clothes remained fundamentally similar until about the middle of the fourteenth century when the whole attitude towards clothes as a convenient covering slowly started to change into one of the keenest competitive objectives of civilization.

FOURTEENTH CENTURY

THERE was no dramatist in France during the fourteenth century whose work approached the quality of that of Adam Le Bossu. French secular farce seemed to lean too heavily in the direction of the personification of the abstract instead of pursuing the advanced tendency, begun during the thirteenth century, towards a lighter vein of very human representation. The last quarter of the century, however, witnessed the constitution of local troupes of players under the name of " Gallants sans Souci."

As yet Spain had no place in the dramatic world. It was not until another century that the theatre began to interest Spanish classic scholars.

Germany, as we know it to-day, was non-existent. The numerous states or countries into which it was divided were so eaten up with their own petty quarrels that civilization was severely retarded and the advance of intelligent research in any direction postponed.

We must turn then to Italy for our inspiration in dramatic work. Here we find the restless and distracted atmosphere recorded for posterity. by Dante. The poet and his age were homogeneous : the winter of barbarism had gone, and the spring of adolescence, with all its accompanying bitterness, had set in. The summer of refinement was yet to come, in the Renaissance. From such periods in history have sprung our greatest geniuses.

It is very probable that there were writers of dramatic farce and works produced on the stage which should rightly belong to the secular theatre, but they must have been so lacking in originality that no reliable information

Fig. 13

has been passed down the centuries regarding them, and they are for ever lost in the mists of obscurity.

The major writers of the age who wrote for the sake of their art were recorders of their contemporary atmosphere, and wrote with no thought of their works being ultimately adapted for the theatre. Nowadays, however, we seem to have reached a stage when practically every dramatic work is being revised for use as a film story or for theatrical production, and if the themes of the Italian fourteenth-century poets are to be utilized in this capacity, it is necessary to have some knowledge of clothing associated with the period.

Petrarch, as well as Dante, has left us valuable dramatic material of this period which might quite reasonably be put on the stage in years to come.

Boccaccio wrote the *Decameron* in 1348, and from these delightful stories was drawn the inspiration of several dramatic works produced during the succeeding centuries.

The story of Griselda, one of these themes, enjoyed much popularity as a playlet in France, was produced in 1395. We find the same story repeated a few years later in Chaucer's *Canterbury Tales*.

It is a very helpful coincidence, therefore, that there appear to be more records of Italian costumes—and particularly those of a more decorative variety—at this particular period (Fig. 13).

There is an inclination on the part of contemporary Italian painters to exaggerate the styles and especially to decorate and pastoralize women's garments, the use of which should be a valuable asset to the producers of works of this time (Fig. 14).

Much discussion has arisen over the Italian artist's representation of woman's crowning glory—the hair.

Fig. 14

Was it really so splendid, or have they idealized it? For our present purpose it is sufficient to record the works of the contemporary artists, as obviously their ideals are conditioned by the realities of the time. While other countries seemed to be doing everything possible to cover women's heads or disguise the hair in such a formal arrangement as to render it almost unrecognizable, Italy made much of it. Plaits and flowing locks crowned with a chaplet of flowers or a plait of hair appear in all their paintings, and a delightful informality and pastoral pleasantness are seen in their gowns (Fig. 15).

The petal shaping at hem and sleeve and the use of the two distinct lengths of gowns, one short with a jagged edge to make a pattern on the contrasting kirtle beneath, give a pleasing variation to an almost stereotyped style of gown worn at that time in other countries.

It will be noticed at once that the Italian man favoured a cap with a hanging top, worn over the coif which had been so popular during the last years of the previous century (Fig. 16). Over the tunic was almost always worn a long gown split up the sides and with hanging sleeves or cape. This garment was popular all over Europe but seemed to have more variety in its cut and arrangement in the Italian interpretation.

The general style of women's gowns, with the exception of Italy, seems to have centred for some forty or fifty years round the rather tight-fitting sleeveless gown, with full-flared skirts. One special feature predominates, this being the new sleeve with the tongue-like finish at the elbow, which was universally adopted as a fashionable feature very early in the century.

After 1350 the sideless surcote exceeded all other styles in popularity. France and the northern countries

Fig. 15

indulged whole-heartedly in competitive battles for the more exaggerated styles.

The French ones appear in most instances to favour a fuller skirt, the folds being gathered into the hip-line in an almost corrugated sequence. The side of the gown being cut very much fuller than the hips themselves, the skirt stood away from the body at the sides, hanging on a sort of curved band attached to the front and back panels. With this arrangement, the tightly fitting kirtle beneath was clearly visible from shoulder to well below the hips, and the girdle, which had become almost a traditional feature of the Middle Ages, was worn balanced on the hip bones and clearly visible through the side openings (Fig. 17).

In both the French and Flemish examples shown here, it will be noticed that the shoulder-yoke and front and back panels were cut all in one piece, the front invariably ornamented with buttons of ornate design which served no useful purpose. The so-called German version of the same garment fits snugly over the hips, and the material of the skirt follows up the line in front; probably this ' strap ' which formed the bodice of the gown was attached in some way to the kirtle beneath, as it is hardly feasible to imagine that the great weight of the skirt could be successfully carried with merely a band of embroidery round the shoulders (Fig. 18).

The figure-fitting gown with full-flared skirts—somewhat shorter than the sideless surcote—and ' fitchets ' (the pocket-like slits that appear in the front of the skirt to enable the wearer to reach the belt underneath, which carried the purse and other paraphernalia of feminine occupation) seemed to be a popular alternative in all European countries (Fig. 19). Details varied, such as the slitting up of the sides of the skirt to show the kirtle beneath,

Fig. 16

Fig. 17

Fig. 18

a rounded or square neckline, both fairly low in cut, and elbow-length sleeves—all with the advantage of displaying the kirtle beneath. These sleeves were either finished with the tongue-like opening, or else with a band of material, often white, wound round the arm and falling in a streamer of varying length, as in Fig. 18. The streamer in Fig. 20A is an entirely decorative arrangement of petals on a tubular pendant.

Tight-lacing is obvious in most of the examples during the second half of the century ; the sharply curved waist-line —with the excessively full skirt splaying out from the hips —tightly fitting sleeves that reach almost to the knuckles, low-cut necklines, and a gracefully hanging semicircular cloak richly lined with furs or contrasting materials form the general basis of outline for some forty years. In colour, contrast seemed to be of primary importance. Parti-coloured gowns were worn a great deal by both men and women, but when this was not done, the idea of the split skirts at the side, the cut-away sides to the gown, the elbow-length sleeves with tippets—all gave ample excuse to display a kirtle of rich design or violently contrasting colour.

While Italian ladies laid out their tresses in all their splendour, the other countries went through numerous experimental stages before eventually breaking out into the wild extravagances of fancy in head-dress witnessed during the closing years of the fourteenth century and throughout the fifteenth century.

During the first thirty or forty years of the fourteenth century, women followed for the most part the established and traditional idea of wimples, barbettes, crespins, etc. (Fig. 21). These fashions were succeeded for some further twenty or thirty years by a formal arrangement of plaits, often

A

B

Fig. 19

A   B

Fig. 20

Fig. 21

tucked into gold casings worn on either side of the circlet. The straight line from forehead to chin was typical of the middle of the century, and its most stylized interpretation occurs in France (Fig. 22). Sometimes a tiny chin veil was worn with this type of hairdressing which gave the head an even more formal and unnatural effect. Sometimes a net of the old jewel-set order was worn over the formally arranged hair, giving the appearance of a bonnet.

The next fashion seems to have had its origin in Germany. This was for a veil with a widely ruched border called a ' Kruseler.' Layers of goffered frills were arranged on the edge that surrounded the face and often at the edge at the back too. These frills fitted closely round the face from forehead to shoulder, and no hair was allowed to show (Figs. 18 and 19).

The general arrangements varied considerably : in some representations the frilly edge seems to wave in and out in imitation of the hair, while in others it has almost the formality of a solid inverted U closely patterned with even pleats.

This inverted U-shape was so popular that one of the earliest forms of ornate head-dress was adapted from it. A solid roll of stuff, covered with mesh and enlivened with jewelled ornaments, was the first of the highly extravagant creations to make its appearance in about 1385.

There seems to be some doubt as to where the peculiar passion for crazy head-dresses originated. So quickly were they adopted and adapted by France, Germany, the Netherlands, and England, that before the close of the fourteenth century the veil and circlet had been generally abandoned, and the ladies indulged their tastes for excess and wild competition in the elaboration of further ornate and bizarre head-dresses.

A   B

Fig. 22

With men's clothes many excesses in brevity and voluminosity took place throughout the century. The inclination towards tight-fitting tunics, remarkable during the closing years of the thirteenth century, was accentuated and exaggerated until a stage had been reached when they had to fasten up in front, so that the seams were not split in struggling into them. Their brevity was the source of continual moralizing and ridicule. Indeed, the loss of the battle of Crécy was attributed to Divine wrath at the indecently and inadequately dressed Frenchmen whose jackets were so short that in bending—to quote a contemporary record—" Any one standing behind them could see their hose as well as the anatomy beneath." The shorter tunics were distinctly a French fashion, which spread with amazing speed to other countries.

About 1340 the low waist-line which had been accentuated by the addition of a heavily jewelled belt, ceased to be absolutely general, normal waist-lines appeared again. This fashion evidently did not supersede the craze for the hip belt, for the latter continued to be popular until the close of the century. The tunic or jacket usually had a flared skirt, except when it was so short that only a few inches appeared below the belt, and this was frequently 'dagged' or cut in a series of points or patterns. There were rows of buttons down the front opening, and often from wrist to elbow. This was the established fashion for many years (Fig 23).

'Dagging' or cutting the edges of sleeves, hems, hoods, etc., was prevalent as early as the 'thirties, but became increasingly popular as the century advanced. The craze became so persistent that longer sleeves, fuller skirts, and more profusely hanging draperies were substituted for the briefer garments for all formal occasions,

A   B

Fig. 23

so that there might be more edges to cut in an increasing variety of shapes (Fig 24). One finds the edges of the gorget and the full hanging sleeves of the super-tunic cut in complicated flower and leaf shapes, and often lined with contrasting material to add to the decorative effect.

At first the fashion pertained almost exclusively to male garments, but later the craze spread to women's fashions and enjoyed a short popularity in feminine circles in the decades surrounding the opening of the fifteenth century.

It was during the last five or ten years of the century that the greatest changes in styles took place. A real interest in clothes as a means of personal expression, fostered by the rapid advancement in the art of tailoring, led to the extravagances and absurdities so typical of the fifteenth century.

The houpelande, a bell-shaped garment fashioned from a complete circle of material, with voluminous hanging sleeves, came into fashion about the year 1385, and remained the almost standardized shape for all male garments for nearly a century. By nature of its shaping no folds appeared on the shoulders, the first fullness was girdled at the waist and from beneath the belt it hung with increasing fullness to the hem. When the houpelande was worn very long it swept in dignified folds on the ground and was usually dagged after the manner of the then prevalent fashion. The sleeves also often swept the ground —an unpractical, but nevertheless effective and imposing fashion.

It was adopted by both men and women and differed little, if at all, in its earliest adaptations. The throat was high, the collar often covering the ears, and it fastened down the front some six or seven inches. Very often the

A   B

Fig. 24

opening at the throat was edged with fur, or the edge of the collar itself might be dagged.

A peculiar fashion which enjoyed a short popularity, and was essentially German in its inception and use, was the passion for bells (Fig. 25). Thus we find bells decorating the hems of tunics, worn round the throat on heavy collars, wired to the belt so that they stood out from the body, and often worn on a chain or wide band of embroidery that was hung from one shoulder across to the opposite hip. There are frequent allusions in contemporary manuscripts to this peculiar fashion, which lasted for some thirty years.

Other excesses of the time include the absurdly elongated toes to the shoes, which produced the usual deluge of abuse that all exaggerated fashions arouse. The extreme brevity of the jackets, the almost wasp-like waists worn by men, the gigantic sleeves which appeared in an astonishing variety of shapes at the beginning of the fifteenth century, and the large bell-like opening to the undersleeve, which almost covered the hand, are other examples.

It is not perhaps surprising that the weird and wonderful head-dresses worn by the women should find their counterpart in those worn by the men. Where previously the hood and the hood reversed had been almost the only form of headgear worn by men, they now broke out into an orgy of extravagant styles, which are, strictly speaking, more typical of the early fifteenth century than the end of the fourteenth.

Fig. 25

FIFTEENTH CENTURY

ALTHOUGH a bewildering mass of material regarding the activities of the French theatre during the fifteenth century exists, the information, though interesting, leaves no definite record of a single praiseworthy work.

In France the whole attitude towards the theatre changed considerably during the Hundred Years' War, and although it had not turned people from patronizing the theatre, it had become once more an instrument for instruction—this time in a political sense more than a religious.

Thus in the year 1494, during the Italian expedition, Charles VIII of France had a play or playlet written and performed with a satirical gibe against the Pope and the King of Spain. The encouragement of the theatre by princes was not because it amused them, but rather because they realized that they might convert it into yet another instrument through which they could extend their power. This attitude is so persistent in the fifteenth-century French farce that it practically ruins any theme that otherwise might be worthy of re-playing.

Fig. 26

Fig. 27

The group of actors most encouraged played in La Sottie—derived from the ancient feast of the Fools of the thirteenth century. The players, wearing green and yellow parti-coloured tunics with dunces' caps on their heads, jeer at all powers—more especially the Church—and outrage any offended person by presenting him with a fool's cap with donkey's ears. This contemporary quotation will show how deep-set was the peculiar enmity to the advancement of the theatre. " . . . What can one do against a scandal which is older than two centuries, and is being practised through all the kingdoms to the great joy of the people ? "

Among this conglomeration of satirical, political, and religious 'digs' no worthy record exists of what might truthfully be called dramatic farce—certainly not dramatic art.

We still find the bands of strolling entertainers frolicking for their own amusement as much as for the amusement of the crowds. These touring companies were gradually ousting the professional jugglers and their traditional paraphernalia of performing animals and theatrical disguises —to be replaced themselves by professional actors who constituted the permanent and temporary travelling troupes of the sixteenth century.

Two so-called Moralities of the century are worth recording, because they had such a long popularity. Produced in 1450, they were still being played as late as 1540. The first, *The History of the Destruction of Troy*, was borrowed from the works of Guido de Colonna, and the second, *Mystery of the Siege of Orleans*, taken from contemporary history.

For the rest, audacious and licentious farce bolstered by buffoonery, bitter satire, and political ridicule robbed

A   B

Fig. 28

the French stage of the fifteenth century of any outstanding work of merit.

Italy again produces the highest degree of literary achievements, and later Spain contributes lavishly to the slowly augmented collection of the fifteenth century.

Bojardo, Lorenzo de Medici, Luigi Pulci, and Ariosto all wrote in a similar manner—that of the rambling romance. The first proceeded to meander to such good purpose that his life's work, *The Loves of Orlando*, was not finished when he died in 1494.

Ariosto, coming after him (born 1474), admired the style of his work to such an extent that he proceeded to enlarge upon Orlando's vicissitudes and adventures and carried on with a kind of sequel to the original theme. This habit of finishing or extending the works of another author seemed to be indulged to a great extent during the fifteenth and sixteenth centuries, as also was the habit of rewriting from another's plot. Besides his *Orlando* he also wrote several plays which were acted in the Court of Alfonso, *Menechino* and *La Cassaria* being his most noteworthy works.

These stories were all highly imaginative, with magic rings, giants, secret potions, and all the fantasy which we may find in the old fairy stories, and it is very probable that Shakespeare took his idea of *A Midsummer Night's Dream* from *The Loves of Orlando*. Here we find the same complexities of the love-blinded youths and maidens wandering through the mazes of an enchanted forest.

Luigi Pulci was another writer of romantic fantasy whose ideas are said to spring from the records of the old chivalrous days written down by Archbishop Turpin during the twelfth century. His greatest work was *Morgante Maggiore*.

Fig. 29

In all these Italian poems we find a pointed wit and airy lightness, which contrasts strangely with the rough humour and extravagant imagination of the Spanish writers.

Juan del Encina wrote the first Spanish plays about 1456. The only earlier attempt in this direction was an allegorical drama written by Villena.

Juan del Encina was born in Salamanca. He travelled to Jerusalem and then lived for some years in Rome, acquiring a knowledge of the Italian dramatists. Curiously enough, his work was not influenced by the Italian style, but followed the romantic tragedy without the hairbreadth escapes and superabundance of magic and supernatural etceteras that typify the Italian writers of the Renaissance.

John I of Aragon invited poets to settle in Barcelona; he also established an academy there for the cultivation of poetry; and at the end of the fifteenth century the theatre began to interest classic scholars. Several of the ancient classics were re-enacted, and a passion for pastoral settings became the vogue.

The first original tragedy published in Spain was the work of Geronimo Bermudez. He wrote *Nisa Lastimosa* and *Nisa Laureada*, both of which were founded on an old Spanish morality play called *Celestina*, whose origin is lost in obscurity. An unwritten version of this play appeared early in the fifteenth century by Fernando de Rojas, and it bears some of the tragedy of young lovers involved in family feuds to be found in *Romeo and Juliet*.

The first few years of the century owe many of their peculiar styles to French and German inspiration (Fig. 31). The gigantic sleeves, small waists, and full skirts worn by the men were repeated by the women, though here, more often than not, the woman's waist-line is high under the breasts,

Fig. 30

while the man's, particularly in Germany and Holland, is still to be found well down on the hips.

The period of exaggerated dagging, pointed toes, huge sleeves, brilliant colouring, and peculiar head-dresses lasted until about the 'thirties. If short, full skirts were not worn by the men they arrayed themselves in the sweeping houpelande and turbaned heads, in silhouette hardly recognizable from their wives and sisters.

The hood, with the face-opening placed on the head —the gorget and liripipe hanging—started to be the most accepted form of male head-dress from the end of the fourteenth century and remained popular for nearly a hundred years. In Fig. 32 four examples have been illustrated to simplify its rather amusing evolution from hood to ' chaperon.'

Fig. *A* shows the hood as worn during the fourteenth century—essentially a garment to protect the head, neck, and shoulders. The edges are dagged round the shoulders in the approved fashion. Fig. *B* shows how the facial opening became the head-opening—the dagged gorgets hanging at one side and the liripipe at the other. In Fig. *C* the liripipe has been wound round the head, lifting the frills made by the hanging gorget and forming a sort of coxcomb on top of the head. A hat was eventually produced to give a somewhat similar effect, though lacking the direct purpose of hood and hat. This hat was called a chaperon or bonnet, and the band that had once been formed by the liripipe became a large turned-up brim; the liripipe was substituted for a ' tippet ' or wide hanging band of material stitched on to the brim of the bonnet, and a bunched length of material with its sides dagged was further added to give the coxcomb effect. The ' tippet ' more often than not was worn under the chin and tucked

Fig. 31

up into the brim the other side of the face, in much the same way that the ladies' barbette of a former age had been arranged with the fillet.   An example of this style can be seen in Fig. 32 *D.*

Not content with this entertaining and varied arrange-

Fig. 32

ment of head-dress, the men indulged in an animated competition in hats of almost every possible conception. Netherlandish styles favoured something very large and made of beaver—the brims were not so large as the crowns—and for some fifty years at least a Flanderish beaver hat was a necessary item in every well-dressed man's wardrobe.

The Italians undoubtedly achieved the most exaggerated fashion of an amazingly grotesque age, some twenty years after the beginning of the century (Fig. 33).

From some of the accompanying drawings one can see that every shape and form was enlarged upon and over-ornamented to such an extent that any original idea of utility was completely overlooked.

Fig. 33

During the 'twenties and 'thirties the full hanging tunics, with their ornate sleeves cut in every conceivable shape and decorated almost out of recognition, practically obliterated the more stately ankle-length garments of a few years earlier.

The bag sleeve with two openings, one at the elbow and one at the extreme end of the sleeve, seemed to be equally popular throughout Europe. But the great cape-

Fig. 34

Fig. 35

sleeve, cut in a half circle of material and stitched in a straight line from shoulder to hem—front and back (see Fig. 34)—was definitely an eccentricity of the Italian Renaissance.

One theme governed the cut of almost every male tunic or surcote—this was the circle. Whether it was cut up the sides or had sleeves added, the same basis was necessary to produce the thickly hanging folds demanded by fashion. Often the sleeveless or sideless garment was girdled in front only, its fullness neatly arranged in pleats from the belt down. Sometimes no belt or girdle was visible, or at least not over the garment; some sort of girdle was necessary to hold the knife and purse, but usually the belt was worn outside—the exact position of the waist varying to suit the wearer's inclination (Fig. 35).

The low waist-line remained popular in Germany some years after the French and Italians had returned to the normal. From knee to mid-thigh was the most popular length for the tunic for the first half of the century—there were of course numerous exceptions, but the very short tunics typical of the closing years of the fourteenth century were not typical of the early fifteenth (Fig. 36).

Later than 1450, however, the silhouette had again changed—first in France this time, to be copied and exaggerated in Italy and Spain. The skirts of the tunic or doublet, as it was now called, were abbreviated to a stage of absurdity reached about 1460 (Fig. 37A). When the full-pleated skirts stood out from the belt only about six inches in length, the waist became tighter and the fullness was arranged across the chest to form an almost feminine curve. The sleeves, from being full at the bottom, were reversed in shape, and all the fullness possible was gathered into the shoulders, the part covering the forearm becoming tight-fitting. This gave the figure the impression of having an absurdly small waist and gigantic shoulders and hips in contrast to the long, slim legs, with their still pointed toes.

At the beginning of the century, men had worn their hair in a variety of 'cuts.' The most usual, and incidentally

Fig. 36

A   B

Fig. 37

the most unattractive, was the style that could be arrived at if a basin were inverted on the head, just touching the top of the ears and the nape of the neck, all the hair that showed beneath this shape being cut away, even to shaving up behind the ears. After about 1420 a 'bob' or long 'bob' with or without a fringe was more popular, and frizzing and curling with irons an everyday occurrence. After the middle of the century the fashion tended towards really long hair—especially in Italy; the style for shoulder-length curls was more general in France (Fig. 38).

Caps with high crowns of varying shapes and little or no brim were worn from the 'sixties to the end of the century, and it is probably from these styles of heads, with their long curls and high hats, that fashion designers of to-day have found their inspiration for so many wild and amusing vogues in women's hats (Fig. 39).

The last forty years of the century saw a variety of brevity and voluminosity in conjunction with each other —no medium measures were countenanced. To be well-dressed, a man must either have his skirts so short that his buttocks were uncovered, which style persistently aroused feverish indignation in certain circles, or else his coat must be long and voluminous with full dignified folds or loosely hanging sleeves (Fig. 40).

Fig. 38

Fig. 39

Fig. 40

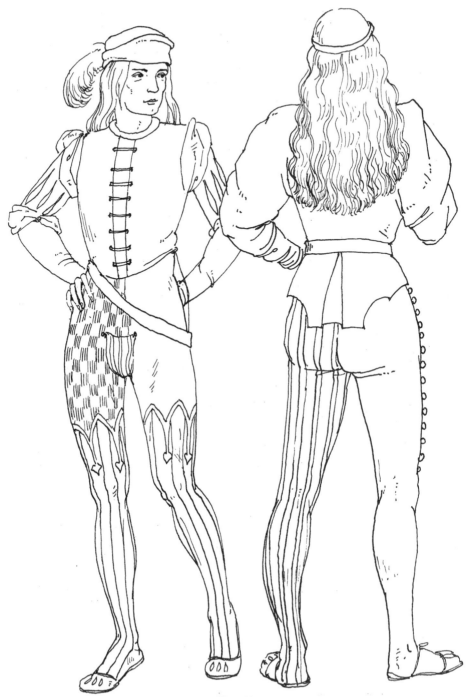

Fig. 41

The extremely brief doublet showed so much of the anatomy, and the hose or tights were so extraordinarily tight-fitting that a pocket front became a necessary feature of these garments, and this was quickly to be replaced by the cod-piece, a peculiarly offensive ex-aggeration which remained in vogue for nearly a century (Fig. 41).

Fifteenth - century design was as different as possible from the smaller themes that had been so popular during the thirteenth and fourteenth centuries. From the very beginning of the century a passion for boldness was predominant in the decoration of all garments. Two of the most popular motifs seemed to be the pomegranate and the pineapple, and these, enlivened by a rich interlacing of leaf designs, appeared in one form or another on both male and female garments. So big were the designs in their execution that at times it was only possible to get one repeat on to a sleeve or front of a garment, and either they were worked on to the garments after they were made up

Fig. 42

or else a great deal of skill and thought was used in their tailoring so that the design appeared evenly matched when the gown or tunic was ready to wear (Fig. 42).

If one bears in mind that fifteenth-century clothes relied on their richness of colour, boldness of design, and exaggeration of shapes, rather than on the barbaric jewelled ornamentation indulged in during the preceding and succeeding centuries, it is perhaps easier to understand the reason for the peculiar persistence of fashionable excesses.

Although the most obvious and therefore more important male garments consisted of hose, doublet, and surcote, a numerous variety of smaller items was added to give the required variety in effect. Separate sleeves were worn from quite early in the century; sometimes they

Fig 43

Fig. 44

were buttoned on at the shoulder, but more often tied with a sort of ornamental shoelace with gold or silver points and threaded through eyelet holes in the two garments. This fashion was commonly known as 'tying with points,' and lasted in favour and general adoption well into the seventeenth century.

The hose were fastened to the gipon or under-tunic in a similar manner, which must have complicated speedy dressing, and caused no little annoyance with its naturally tightened knots after a hard day's work or sport.

The glimpses of the under-garments caused by this method of fastening necessitated the use of finer linen, and the use of finer linen appeared to spur the wearers on to further excuses for displaying it. Thus we find numerous fashions introduced with this purpose in view: sleeves slit from wrist to elbow, and tied at intervals; the fronts of doublets split to the waist and the shirt puffed out like a pouter-pigeon; and lacings crossing the front opening to add pattern

Fig. 45

And during the last years of the century the introduction of slashing supplied the excuse for endless excess in this direction (Fig. 44).

So much for the men, then. The century had opened to the jingling of German bells, to cropped heads, long toes, huge bell-shaped sleeves, small waists, and collars and cuffs covering the lobes of the ears or the knuckles of the fingers, in their bell-like shapings true to the tinkling tradition of the times. It passed on from the heavy drapings, rich colourings, and expensive beaver and furs of the Burgundian Courts to the fantastic and distorted shapes of the Italian Renaissance, with their exaggerated hats and ribbons, pleats and curls, frills and feathers, and finally aroused a keenly national com-

Fig. 46

petitive attitude towards dress in all European countries (Fig. 45). The slashings and puffings of the German Courts vied with the gilded draperies of the Italian and Spanish. The French fashions fostered a passion for subtle tailoring which earned for Parisian couturièrs a long-established name for perfection of cut.

The simplicity of feminine attire (Fig. 46)—which had until a few years before the fifteenth century been an established feature—had vanished finally in an avalanche of new modes and an obvious desire to compete with the varied styles of the men, soon after the century began.

Trains were perhaps the most obvious excess of the century. Gowns became not only inches but yards longer. A modish style prevented any easy movement of the limbs, and unless the skirts were gathered up in front, walking became impossible—here we see the reason for all the contemporary ladies of the early and middle fifteenth century being depicted with masses of skirt bunched up in front and held over the stomach (Fig. 47). It was, without doubt, the only way to facilitate movement, and the amount of material in these skirts is only possible to estimate if it is realized that they were practically always circular in cut, therefore the yard or so that usually rested on the ground was some ten times the circumference of the folds about the waist.

The two most obvious fashions in dress for fifty years or more were the sideless surcote and the houpelande (Fig. 48). With the latter the variety in sleeves was as complicated and numerous as in those of the men—but its original shaping as a complete bell from the shoulder changed considerably until we find versions with the top fitting the body closely without folds to the waist, and the bell-shape from the waist down (Fig. 49).

Fig. 47

Fig. 48

Fig. 49

The sideless surcote remained fundamentally the same until the 'sixties, and the sleeves of the kirtle beneath were always tight-fitting.

A style which appears to have arisen as a result was that of a figure-fitting garment from shoulder to hip; this was richly decorated and was often sideless, but always tight-fitting, low-necked, and short-sleeved, so that it might show the garments beneath. It appears to have been worn mostly in Germany (Fig. 50).

Throughout the century one style found undiminishing favour; this was of the closely fitting gown which flared out from the hips in a bewildering fullness. Its sleeves might follow any known and approved style, and occasionally a girdle was worn with it; otherwise the same gown might have been worn for some seventy years.

During the last decade of the century the whole style altered. The curved clinging lines of the Middle Ages gave place to the high-waisted and full-gathered skirts which have become in most instances the inspiration of traditional national costumes of the various European countries. It was undoubtedly from these particular decades in history that many of the peasant costumes have come (Fig. 52). The peculiar head-dresses which are now symbolical of certain countries were probably fashionable only for some twenty or thirty years, but their very ornateness and expense have rendered them traditional. The ladies who first wore them so valued these pieces of extravagant indulgence that they were handed down with care to their children and children's children to be worn only on feast-day and special occasions. Eventually when time had begun to render them all but shabby and dilapidated, they were almost an established feature of gala days and had to be reproduced in all their sparkling glory, replicas

Fig. 50

of an age long dead, but nevertheless still a cherished fashion.

These head-dresses of the fifteenth century stand out in the history of costume as perhaps the most noticeable and arresting peculiarity.

There seemed to be no end to their variations and eccentricities, and to give a full description of each and every style would be, after five hundred years, an impossibility, for each lady of fashion devised new methods of adorning the standard shapes which by about 1420 were very numerous. There were the rolled head-dress, resembling in shape an enormous dough-nut ring; the steeple, hennin, or sugar-loaf, with its tall point and flowing veil; the butterfly, composed of a complicated arrangement of folded and stiffened lawn or linen of elegant transparency; the box head-dress which, when completed in shape, resembled two large flower-pots—one over each ear, covered with gold mesh and jewels, and usually surmounted by a crown and veil; the horned head-dress, gigantic and unwieldy, or small and compact; the great U-shaped roll, with decorated sides and spangled veil; the one of Egyptian shape that was

Fig. 51

Fig. 52

Fig. 53

curiously reminiscent of Queen Nefertitis; the slightly
tapering black cylinder complete with eye-veil; the
dozens of German and Dutch nun-like head and face
drapings (Fig. 53).

And to make up in some part for the lack of jewellery

A

B

C

D

Fig. 54

worn on their gowns, the majority of these head-dresses
abounded in rich and exotic decoration; gold lacings,
pearls, and gem ornaments were arranged in complicated
patterns or studded carelessly here and there to suit the
vagaries of the wearers. Transparent lawn played a very
important part in the majority of these head-erections.

Long sweeping veils or tiny stiffened eye-veils were usually worn when the head-dress itself was not entirely composed of this material.

The majority of these head-dresses are comparatively easy to reconstruct with the aid of buckram, tulle, and wire, but lacking the first material it is very difficult to imagine how these formidable erections retained their shape during the fifteenth century (Fig. 54). On a close study of some of the heads of the contemporary memorials and effigies, their construction gives the impression of metal work rather than any more flexible composition. It is quite probable that quite a number of the more ornate erections were composed of a gilded and jewelled wire cage, lined with some rich silk material. When this was the case their weight must have been no small consideration.

With all these head-dresses the most remarkable and general feature is the complete lack of any hair showing. This freakish fashion was so persistently prevalent that the ladies went so far as to pluck the hair from their foreheads and necks so that not a single stray lock might be visible to detract from the majesty or peculiarity of their head-dressing.

This fashion gave the ladies an unnatural stiffness and formality, and worn in conjunction with the sweeping trains and finger-tip length sleeves accentuated the white oval of the face and the slim column of the neck.

One notices their hairless effect both in the nude and draped figures of the period; the hair being so dragged back and shaved from the forehead that the women appear to have peculiarly bulging foreheads and a rather masculine baldness about their faces, and the hair from being perpetually packed away beneath a weighty head-dress falls in long, creeping strands, lank and lifeless.

Fig. 55

At this period fashions catered with equal thought for young and old. The soft folds of the wimple and butterfly or nun-like head-dress softened the relaxing outlines of the older woman's face and gave dignity and quality to those who had lost the first freshness of youth (Fig. 55).

Fig. 56

In much the same way the chaperon and hood, with the flowing gowns worn by the more sedate and elderly men, instead of attempting to compete with the long-legged brevity and jaunty hat of youth, inspired a dignity of their own.

It is a great pity that other ages have not been so accommodating with their styles. Youth and age should not compete or try to wear the same fashions.

The peculiarly excessive modes in head-dressing had almost vanished by 1490, and a complete revulsion in styles had welcomed once more the fashion for long hair.

During the 'eighties several German fashions followed the Italian method of introducing the hair into the head-

A   B   C

Fig. 57

dress, but there is a hardness and almost brutal treatment in their stiffly plaited heads, which is certainly lacking in the informal 'formality' of the Italian fashions. This is particularly noticeable in Figs. 52 and 56.

Throughout the fifteenth century, when all the other European countries vied with one another to make their women appear bald, the Italians continued to allow their hair to show (Fig. 57). Even with the more severe styles we can still see tiny wisps of curls peeping insolently from beneath the head-dress, and numerous methods were adopted and adapted so that a fashion worn in other countries might be worn in Italy without the necessity of covering the wearer's luxuriant tresses. Even with the horned head-dress we may see instances of the hair being drawn through the horns and falling in waves and curls from the points, while in the other European versions, a veil would answer the purpose (Fig. 58).

Fig. 58

It has been suggested that fondness for depicting hair shown by the Italian and some Spanish artists, during a period traditionally famous for its hairless beauties, was merely the artist's personal aversion to the extinguishing of women's crowning glory, and that he compelled his models to abandon their fantastic head-dresses in favour of a more pastoral effect which he himself engineered in his studio only.

Fig. 59

On a minute study of the numerous works of contemporary artists, this suggestion does not appear practical. The same coincidence could not possibly occur on all the pieces of sculpture, portraiture, and illustration (Fig. 59). The same or similar arrangements of hair could hardly be a figure of each and every Italian painter's imagination painted at different dates in different parts of the country. It is more than probable, however, that one or two artists—Botticelli, for instance—preferred to rearrange their models

Fig. 60

Fig. 61

and make more of their hair than they were in the habit of wearing for everyday occasions (Fig. 60). Some of Botticelli's complex arrangements of plaits and pearls appear a trifle too ornate to be feasible.

It most certainly appears, therefore, that Italian women did not favour the French and German fashions that completely eclipsed their hair (Fig. 61). If a high head-dress was the fashion, then the hair must play a part in it—and numerous very charming and amusing styles, many of which have been included in these pages, were the ultimate result.

SIXTEENTH CENTURY

ALTHOUGH there were brilliant works by many dramatists, and general experiments in a more finished theatrical production throughout the fifteenth century, the sixteenth offers much more in this direction. And this time Spain contributes more to dramatic records than any other country.

Lope de Rueda constructed the paraphernalia of a dramatic actor and manager in the very simple form of a large bag, its contents consisting of " Four white dresses for shepherds, trimmed with copper gilt ; four sets of false beards and wigs ; and four crooks." The average comedies could all be played with these properties, as at that time the themes varied little from conversations between shepherds and shepherdesses, with a negro chorus.

Lope de Rueda, who was an actor as well as a dramatic manager, has been termed the founder of the Spanish theatre, but it is perhaps to Naharro this title should belong, as he instituted dramatic effects in thunderstorms, noises off for battles, etc., a sidescreen with cloud effects, and an orchestra in front of the stage. And with these added attractions came a reaction from the false beards, and a greater demand for better stage-properties, which resulted in the abandonment of the bag in favour of large boxes containing a greater selection of clothes.

During the sixteenth century dramas were acted all over Western Europe, and the establishment of repertory troupes became a feature of numerous large towns.

It was with considerable difficulty that the theatre, as a public entertainment, established itself in Spain.

A   Fig. 62   B

Though as a court amusement it was undeniably popular.

Among the many brilliant dramatists of the sixteenth century, Lope de Vega appears to have been the most prolific in his productions, although out of nine hundred plays written by him only a few remain. Possibly a great number followed the fashion of the time and were stories told in dialogue, with various scene-changes.

Cervantes, born in 1547, wrote *Don Quixote*, the most successful book in the history of Spain. He tried throughout his lifetime to rectify the deficiencies of the stage, and some idea of the appreciation of the general public may be gathered from his statement: " I wrote at that time some twenty or thirty plays, which were all performed without the public throwing pumpkins or oranges or any of these things which spectators are apt to cast at the heads of bad actors. My plays were acted without hissing, confusion, or clamour."

The theme of *Don Quixote* seems to have originated from Mendoza's *Lazarillo de Tormes*, which was written about 1530. With all these plays and stories the original appeared in some form or other several years before the now known version.

Jorge de Montemayor, 1520–61, another Spanish writer, among other works wrote *Diana*, an acted pastoral which established a Spanish fashion, approved and imitated by practically every other Spanish poet of the time. Cervantes' *Galatea* and, later, Shakespeare's *Cymbeline* and *The Winter's Tale*, all appear to have been inspired by this delightful *Diana*.

The craze for pastoral themes ousted for a time all the stories of romantic chivalry which had been so popular during the preceding century.

Fig. 63

Fig. 64

Fig 65

In Italy the same preference occurred, and with the possible exception of Tasso's *Rinaldo*, which once more carried on with the now time-worn version of *Orlando*, the majority of Italian writers accepted the pastoral influences of Spain.

Andreas Hartman, a German, wrote a comedy in five acts, published in 1587, which appears to be about the only play written in Germany during the sixteenth century. After numerous struggles in this direction, the only significant and visible result emerging from the close of the sixteenth century was the establishment of the theatre in Germany.

The fashion for slashing that had been noticeable during the closing years of the fifteenth century now became an exaggerated motif in all fashionable apparel (Fig. 65). In Italy the style found its way into sleeves more than any other part of the clothing. These became a complicated collection of small pieces held together with 'points' or jewelled fastenings, and from each curved and cut portion of sleeve projected voluminous puffings of the under-sleeve, which was made in very liberal proportions. A square *décolleté* neck was almost as universal as the V's had been a few years earlier, and once more an over-adornment of chains and necklaces, ear-rings and brooches, was the fashion. In less than twenty years, 1485–1500, all traces of the medieval influence of ornate head-dresses and flowing circular skirts had completely vanished in favour of the high-waisted gathered skirt, slashed and bunched sleeves, and an entirely new method in head-tyring, where each country favoured its own styles (Fig. 66).

In Germany and Holland the bonnet or cap, tight-fitting round the face and bulging into a globular shape at the back of the head, was most popular for several years (Figs. 67

Fig. 66

Fig. 67

and 68). Italy preferred hats of a masculine type. France adapted several charming styles which were in a great measure imitated by other countries—the hair was often worn in a chignon (Fig. 69). A band of linen worn over the head, falling down either side of the face almost to the shoulders and often decorated with gems, was the foundation of many styles. Over this could be worn a veil, often lined with a contrasting material and split at the back; a variety of fashions emerged from the arrangement of this (Fig. 70). One particular mode which appears to have been only worn in France was the arrangement of a head-dress so that it appeared as a curved X on top of the head (Fig. 71).

Spanish styles preferred a simple arrangement, and often the only ornament on the hair was an elegant net with the hair bunched up inside (Fig. 72). The difference between hats and head-dresses is very apparent throughout the sixteenth century—a head-dress was essentially a feminine decoration, but the hat might be worn by either men or women, and we find identical hats worn by both sexes throughout the entire century. There are, indeed, many instances when a man's head might easily be taken for a woman's, and *vice versa*. Low-cut neck-lines and the flowing locks and large beaver hats of Italian and Germanic origin do much to destroy the usual obvious contrasts.

What the ladies' dresses acquired in volume, the men's

Fig. 68

Fig. 69

Fig. 70

Fig. 71

Fig. 72

most certainly outbalanced in their extreme brevity—at least for some fifteen or twenty years after the beginning of the century.

Absurdly abbreviated doublets—in some cases having the appearance of a tiny sleeveless bodice—were cut away here and cut away there, with a low square neck, a wide gap between the fastenings in the front, and detachable sleeves, all giving excellent excuses for displaying the gorgeousness of their fine embroidered linen beneath (Fig. 73).

Germany carried this mode to extravagant excesses in her wild adventures in the field of slashing. In some cases it is unbelievable that these much-slashed garments could have stayed together at all. We see the legs of hose cut in every conceivable direction, great segments of linings pulled out of hardly connected severings (Fig. 74). Later, as the fashion became more established, numerous methods were devised in which the same or similar effects could be produced without the necessity of cutting to quite such an extent, and, later still, tiny slashings were imitated by little puffs of material sewn on to a perfectly whole garment. Ribbons were used a great deal to give much the same effect.

No single item of apparel escaped the snippings of the tailors' shears. Gloves were ornately slashed so that a bulge might appear on every knuckle with the stretchings of the slashed leather; patterns were cut out on the gauntlets of these same gloves. Shoes became a mere apology for a foot-covering. The pointed toes worn for hundreds of years completely vanished before the beginning of the sixteenth century, and in their place appeared a mule-like square-toed slipper, the toe cut in various patterns and evenly slashed from toe to instep (Fig. 75). There might be a tiny covering for the heel tied with a leather thong round the ankle, or the entire sole from toe-cap to heel

Fig 73

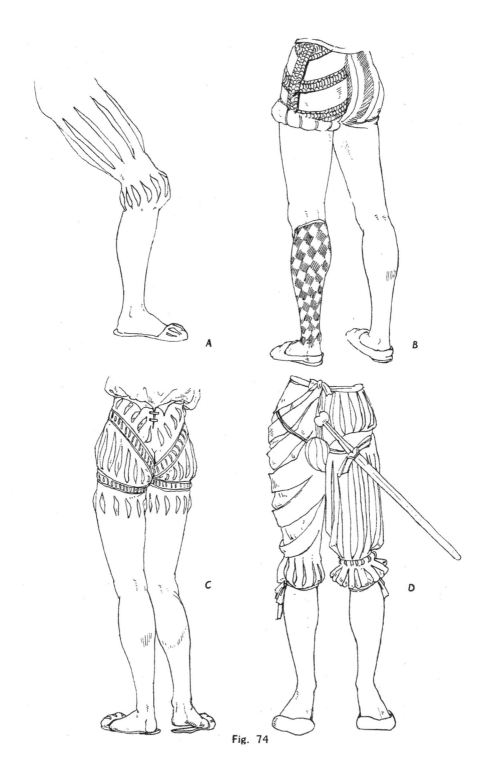

Fig. 74

Fig. 75

might be unattached, the wearer being compelled to keep his shoes on more by knack than anything else.

Hats were slashed, and we find many amusing styles arising from this fashion. Should the brim be cut at intervals of three or four inches, some of the pieces might be folded back against the brim and an endless variety of shapes could be designed.

While Germany made numerous experiments in an intriguing variety of ornate slashings with abbreviated doublets, immense sleeves, and fantastically tattered hose, France added a skirt to the short-waisted doublet, and with the lavishness typical of the period, produced a garment with skirts almost as fully pleated as those worn by the women. This style was adopted by Italy and carried to further extremes, until in some representations we see the men's skirts standing out almost like a ballet skirt (Fig. 77). Italian styles still favoured stripes, and these new skirts were often made of alternate colourings and worn over striped hose. The extreme tightness of the short doublet and the exaggerated fullness of all sleeves were the two typical features of the first twenty years of the century.

The fashion for skirts on men's doublets was not entirely universal, and as early as 1530 we see the Spanish styles turning towards a long, straight doublet reaching below the waist, and what had been the slashed hose turning into the trunk-hose typical of the sixteenth century. As the peculiar passion for slashings abated somewhat, a sort of compromise was made in the decoration of the hose. Only vertical slashings were used, and these usually appeared from mid-thigh to the hip. The linings were drawn out, and the original length of the ribbon-like slashing exaggerated, until soon after 1530 trunk-hose

A   Fig. 76   B

Fig. 77

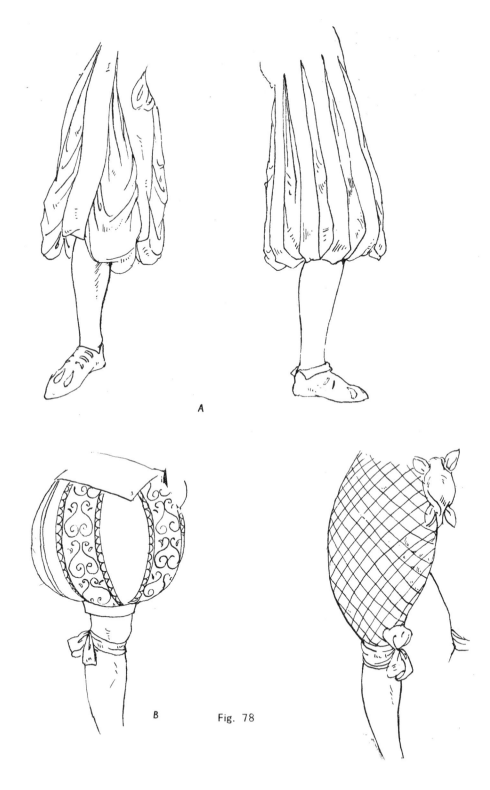

A

B   Fig. 78

appeared. Gradually the linings to these garments assumed more and more voluminous proportions, until eventually stuffings of rags or horsehair were inserted, so that an almost pumpkin-like rotundity appeared surrounding the hips and thighs and making sitting down an exceedingly difficult accomplishment (Fig. 78). The various ways in which this fashion was interpreted by different countries at corresponding dates is very interesting and amusing. The German styles dispensed with the bombasting as much as possible, their particular forms of exaggeration being the vast quantities of stiff and crackly silk used in the linings. These were drawn out and fell in great voluminous folds between the strips of original material, often almost to the ankle. The linings were also hitched and arranged over the lower sword belt and the strap that held the dagger or powder horn (Fig. 79).

These peculiar nether-garments were commonly alluded to as ' plunder-hose,' as they were a style adapted at first by the Swiss and German mercenaries. Their title was apt in more ways than one, for certainly these voluminous garments made an excellent storage place for plundered goods, though their origin seems to have been from hose that had been plundered, slashed in this absurd fashion to fit the new owners, and stuffed with the rich materials discovered among other treasures. It is said that in walking, these plunder-hose made a sort of ' frou-frou ' sound very much admired and encouraged by the followers of the mode. In the majority of the French styles the upper-stocks were filled tightly and neatly, at first resembling in contour two footballs from hip to mid-thigh, but later when the upper- and netherstocks were joined, the bombasting appeared in an almost unbroken single roll worn just round the hips.

Fig. 79

The doublet in Germany remained short-waisted and skirted for some fifteen years or more after the long-waisted Spanish styles had been introduced, and during this period, 1530–45, we find the most marked contrasts in the fashions of the north and south. The only garment which appeared fundamentally the same was the wide-shouldered gown, fur-lined, with fantastic hanging sleeves and deep, wide collar from shoulder to hem. This gown was universally popular for some fifty years and varied only in its length and decoration.

As with the men, German women favoured the high-waisted type of gown. Full pleated skirts, high necks, and a curved corset and bulging sleeves were worn, with a tiny bonnet or jaunty masculine cap set on one side of the head (Fig. 80 and 81).

Spanish and Italian ladies had lowered their waist-lines, corseted themselves in leather from breast to hips, split up their skirts to display a gorgeous underskirt or petticoat, and generally assumed the silhouette more typical of the 1550's, soon after 1530. Gigantic sleeves with a bell-shaped opening did much to disguise the V-shaped corset, but this passion for tight-lacing and un-natural stiffness typifies the Spanish ladies throughout the remainder of the century. Although the stomacher or stiff bodice became considerably longer and even more re-straining in shape during the years after 1550, the silhouette, except for the addition of the ruffle, changed very little in Spain, once this style was established.

French styles favoured a waist-line almost normal, and their chief differences were still in the matter of head-dressing. Their coifs and cauls were entirely different from the modes of either Germany, Spain, or Italy (Fig. 82).

The increasingly full skirts worn in Spain soon de-

Fig. 80

A   B

Fig. 81

manded some sort of foundation to hold them up, and we find the first of the crinoline ideas in the Spanish farthingale or vertingale, introduced a few years before the middle of the century. The craze was universally adopted, and all sorts of contrivances of stiffening and hoops were arranged to keep the skirts out in the fashionable bell-shape. The favourite method seemed to consist of a hoop of material at the bottom of the petticoat and a crescent-shaped roll of padding worn tied round the waist beneath the skirt.

The ruffles which had slowly been forming from the tightly gathered edges of the skirt or shift were first seen in Holland, their rich shining curves assisted by the novel discovery of starch. These ruffles were a deep creamy shade. It is not only the age of the portraits of some old Dutch masters that gives the whites such a rich, yellow tinge ; it was the true representation of the starched caps and bonnets and ruffles, the earlier starches all having a slightly yellow tinge which was later substituted by blue. This discovery of starch facilitated the making up of caps, bonnets, collars, cuffs, and aprons, and in consequence these items received more and more attention until eventually they materialized into the fantastic lace affairs worn throughout Europe at the end of the century.

Fig. 82

Women's sleeves echoed the contour of men's legs during the 'fifties—a full-padded sleeve worn from shoulder to midway between the elbow and armpit terminated in a close-fitting sleeve to the wrist. This style was French in inspiration but was so quickly adopted that very few sleeves worn during the 'sixties did not follow the fashion (Fig. 83).

It must be remembered throughout this period, 1500–1550, that the gowns and kirtles, petticoats and stomachers, did not complete the ladies' entire wardrobe. Numerous small garments, such as odd sleeves, tiny shoulder capes, and false fronts to show where the skirt split up the front, were utilized to add to the general effect of luxury and wealth.

The century made an ostentatious display of personal possessions. Gigantic sums were squandered on clothes and the various items that went to their adornment. Buttons particularly were a much coveted possession, and where these did not form the theme for a decoration, pearls, jewels, embroideries, and slashings of microscopic dimensions took their place (Fig. 84).

Fantastic as the clothes of the first half of the sixteenth century were, those styles worn during the second half rivalled them in every essential feature. Every possible exaggeration of shape took place during this period, and no other fifty years in history saw so many changes in the shaping of men's nether garments.

Full bombasted knee-breeches tied at the knees with a large flowing garter were favoured in Italy soon after the 'sixties; and a few years later another Italian style appeared where the trunk-hose were severed at the knee and another stocking worn over or under them which just covered the knee or reached to mid-thigh (Fig. 85). This gave the legs

Fig. 83

Fig. 84

Fig. 85

three separate kinds of material—first the roll at the hips, still split or composed of strips over the bombasted linings ; then the appendage from mid-thigh to below the knees, which might consist of almost any material but more often than not was made of ' tricot,' the earliest form of jersey cloth; and then the ' nether-stocks,' or short hose gartered at the knees. The absurdly slashed trunk-hose, with hanging linings of liberal proportion, were still worn a great deal in Germany and France. Germany, indeed, favoured these styles until the close of the century, though France was quick to adopt the Italian styles. Towards the 'eighties, however, France had a style of her own; this was for an ' open-breecher,' a somewhat clumsy form of which we should now call ' shorts ' finishing just below the knees. Endless variations of these styles occurred all over Europe (Fig. 86).

The doublet, once generally established as a long-waisted garment with a short skirt and padded chest, started to swell to alarming proportions over the stomach. It would appear that here again its origin was in the Venetian courts, as the most exaggerated styles are to be found in Italian prints (Fig. 87). This hideous and deforming fashion was also adopted by Italian ladies, and many scandalous and ribald suggestions were hurled at the followers of so ungainly a fashion. The craze reached its absurd climax during the 'eighties, and after that slowly abated in size until merely a faint echo of its original form appears in the 'nineties. The shoulders were exaggerated throughout this period—epaulets and rolls were added when the sleeve itself was not very full, and ruffles increased in size and decoration until the close of the century (Fig. 88).

The heavily furred and gathered gown worn during

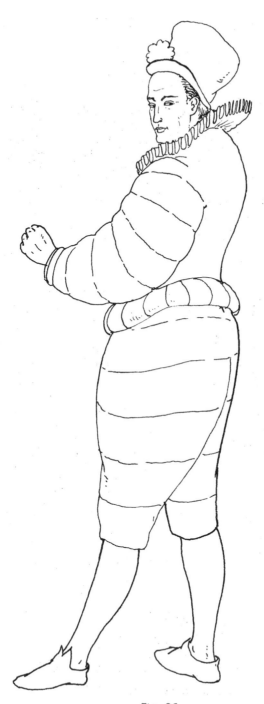

Fig. 86

Fig. 87

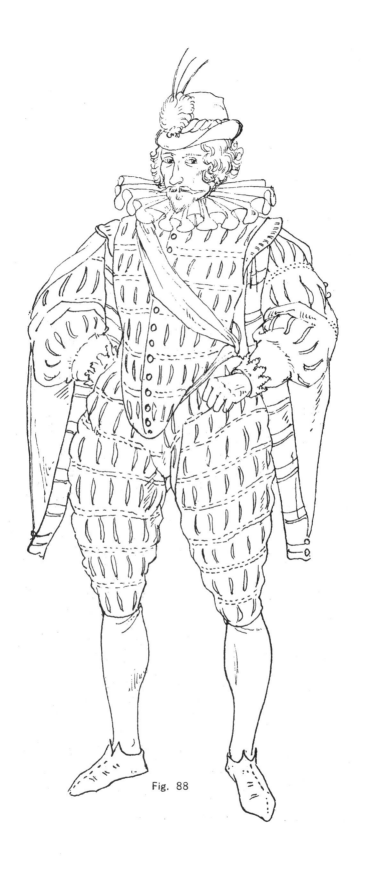

Fig. 88

the first half of the century was gradually succeeded by the Spanish fashion for capes, and the French one for ' mandilions,' or short coats with hanging sleeves.

Beards and moustaches were generally popular, but this again was a Spanish style.

Hats were so many and varied that it is impossible to trace their original wearer—Spain, Venice, or France. Germany was very much the laggard follower in the bewildering game of quickly changing styles (Fig. 89).

The German ladies, however, branched out in their own interpretation of the prevailing styles ; and following the general tendency to unnatural stiffness, in effect attained a percentage of this without the obvious discomfort of the steel and leather straight-lacing of Spain. Though their skirts were full and stiffened, and their coats stood stiffly away from their bodies, their figures were allowed to curve as Nature intended, and the waist-line remained at the waist-line or even higher, while other countries were indulging in the V-shaped stomacher (Fig. 90).

Spanish ladies tightened their corsets and elongated their stomachers, the demand of fashion desiring that the front silhouette should be completely flat from the breast down-wards. Iron hoops were worn in the bell-shaped skirts, and gigantic starched lace ruffles permitted little freedom in head-movement. The hair had to be piled high upon the head so that the ruffle did not interfere with its delicate arrangement of pearls and jewels, wreaths and borders.

France, not to be outdone by Spanish exaggeration (Fig. 91), perpetuated her own especial species of torture for her fair followers of fashion ; this with the introduction of the French vertingale—a huge hoop to be worn round the hips and tilted down in the front, giving the figure the effect of a huge cheese cut slantwise across the top,

A   B   C

Fig. 89

Fig. 90

I. GERMAN (1260)

Vol. 1 (facing p. 18)

II. GERMAN (1300)

Vol. 1 (facing p. 34)

III. ITALIAN (1340)

Vol. 1 (facing p. 42)

IV. ITALIAN (1370)

Vol. 1 (facing p. 50)

V. SPANISH (1414)

Vol. 1 (facing p. 58)

VI. ITALIAN (1440)

Vol. 1 (facing p. 78)

VII. FLEMISH (1460)

Vol. 1 (facing p. 86)

VIII. FRENCH (1480)

Vol. 1 (facing p. 92)

FRENCH

ITALIAN

GERMAN

FLEMISH

IX. FRENCH, ITALIAN, GERMAN, AND FLEMISH (1460)

Vol. 1 (facing p. 98)

X. ITALIAN (1494)

Vol. 1 (facing p. 102)

XI. GERMAN (1505)

Vol. 1 (facing p. 110)

XII. GERMAN (1538)

Vol. 1 (facing p. 118)

XIII. ITALIAN (1533)

Vol. 1 (facing p. 126)

XIV. FRENCH (1570)

Vol. 1 (facing p. 130)

XV. SPANISH (1585)

Vol. 1 (facing p. 136)

XVI. FRENCH (1599)

Vol. 1 (frontispiece)

I. DUTCH (1620)

Vol. 2 (facing p. 28)

II. FRENCH (1630)

Vol. 2 (facing p. 34)

III. DUTCH (1660)

Vol. 2 (facing p. 44)

IV. FRENCH (1670)

Vol. 2 (facing p. 60)

V. FRENCH (1680)

Vol. 2 (facing p. 72)

VI. FRENCH (1700)

Vol. 2 (facing p. 86)

VII. FRENCH (1710)

Vol. 2 (facing p. 92)

VIII. FRENCH (1727)

Vol. 2 (facing p. 98)

IX. FRENCH (1745)

Vol. 2 (facing p. 102)

X. GERMAN (1760)

Vol. 2 (facing p. 110)

XI. FRENCH (1765)

Vol. 2 (frontispiece)

XII. FRENCH (1774)

Vol. 2 (facing p. 118)

XIII. GERMAN (1794)

Vol. 2 (facing p. 124)

XIV. FRENCH (1795)

Vol. 2 (facing p. 128)

XV. FRENCH (1815)

Vol. 2 (facing p. 134)

XVI. FRENCH (1840)

Vol. 2 (facing p. 142)

Fig. 91

Fig. 92

A   B   C

Fig. 93

with the absurdly laced stomacher like a V balanced in the centre. Wide shoulders exaggerated the top of the V, and the sleeves were bombasted and stuffed into a sausage-like contour (Fig. 92). Although the ruffles were of proportions as absurd as those of the Spanish styles, the hair was not dressed in the same manner. Pads were worn at the side of the head, and the hair laid out and arranged to form a heart-shape round the face.

Venetian ladies, as already mentioned, adopted the revolting stuffed and padded bodice worn by men, and their hair was arranged in even more fantastic shapes, two horns being necessary for the fashionable lady (Fig. 93). Not only did the Italian styles differ in hairdressing and the shaping of the bodice, but the ruffle in its full circular shaping never became really popular. High ' Medici' collars were always more typical, and a thick short bodice succeeded the fashion for a padded stomach. Skirts, too, though full, did not stand out, either in the bell-shape dear to Spanish ladies or the cheese-shaped farthingale inseparable from the French courts of the 'eighties and 'nineties (Fig. 94).

Slashing as a decoration was more popular in Spain and Venice than in France. Minute puffs appear all over the ladies' garments. They were probably superimposed, but they nevertheless produced the desired effect (Fig. 95).

Dutch and Flemish ladies' chief fancy was for ruffles and caps. Gigantic ruffles and stiffly starched domed caps top their rather peasant-like forms. Their colder winters demanded the wearing of long full coats.

The art of design or pattern during this century progressed in leaps and bounds. In fact, it appears that practically every garment was especially constructed so that it might be an excellent background for the designer's whims.

Fig. 94

The early years of the century were perhaps a trifle too much occupied with the intriguing arrangement of slashings, jewelled clasps and buttons, and bands of contrasting materials to indulge very much in other forms of pattern, but presently even these excitements became more amusing when garnished by patterns on or surrounding them.

With the advancement of weaving and block-printing, the endless possibilities of damask effects were exploited, and chain patterns were introduced on every possible surface too small for a bolder design.

The century ended with a flood of attempted realism, strangely out of keeping with the peculiar shapes that it had to adorn. Practically all the materials were embroidered or woven with designs of flowers, fruit, fish, or fowl, or indeed any other familiar object that presented itself to the artist's mind.

Fig. 95

ILLUSTRATED HANDBOOK OF
WESTERN EUROPEAN
COSTUME

THIRTEENTH TO MID-NINETEENTH CENTURY

VOLUME TWO: SEVENTEENTH TO MID-NINETEENTH CENTURY

ILLUSTRATED HANDBOOK OF
WESTERN EUROPEAN
COSTUME

Thirteenth to Mid-Nineteenth Century

TWO VOLUMES BOUND AS ONE

VOLUME TWO: SEVENTEENTH TO MID-NINETEENTH CENTURY

Iris Brooke

DOVER PUBLICATIONS, INC.
Mineola, New York

CONTENTS

ILLUSTRATIONS

PLATES IN COLOUR*

ILLUSTRATIONS IN THE TEXT

*For this edition, all the color plates are bound together between pages 144 and
145 of Volume One. Their original page positions appear above.

INTRODUCTION

BY the beginning of the seventeenth century the theatre was a recognized amusement of kings and princes throughout Western Europe. And although still regarded with disfavour by the Church, it was a sufficiently established feature to be the inspiration of the cleverest and most gifted writers of the day. In this manner the present volume differs from its forerunner. Whereas, in the first volume, all authors whose work might ultimately be altered or adapted for theatrical production were mentioned, as actual playwrights were few, in the period covered by this, the most gifted and accomplished writers of the time had turned their attention to the writing of plays, with all the fervour and enthusiasm aroused by a new outlet for dramatic talent.

As every notable artist or author has had hundreds of lesser brains who strove to mimic and copy his themes and subjects, style and technique, so each playwright of original ideas and unusual outlook has had his satellites. And although the names mentioned in these pages are comparatively few, there are numerous inferior but similar writers of every period in every country, so numerous indeed, that it would be impossible to discuss even their most meritorious works in a slender volume like this. It must follow, then, that only those dramatic authors of admitted brilliance and leadership have been mentioned, and only their most famous works catalogued. The purpose of this book is mainly to depict costume in accurate detail. Its relationship to the stage is of secondary importance to its actual value as a record of contemporary fashions and features.

We get four distinct types of theatrical amusement during the seventeenth and eighteenth centuries—the Italian Commedia dell' Arte, the Spanish drama, French heroic tragedies, and light comedies and ballet.

The Commedia dell' Arte—or the Italian Comedians—consisted of troupes of wandering players, each figure with a traditional name and costume. Their plots were for the most part thin and futile ; their success relied entirely on the ludicrous representation of human follies and weaknesses. Parts were not learned, for each actor improvised as the play progressed, but the characters nevertheless became familiar and well-beloved figures. Their vulgar and coarse buffoonery was everywhere welcomed by the people as a pleasant and amusing distraction. As their popularity increased towards the end of the seventeenth century several playwrights endeavoured to introduce similar comic figures into their own works.

In Spain drama was rich with violent and blood-curdling excitements, swashbuckling coarseness, and enthralling love-interests. The Moorish strain lent colour to these exciting dramas, and the voyages and the conquests of Spanish history provided absorbing and fascinating themes.

The French tragedies were a curious mixture of pseudo-Greek and Roman fiction and contemporary fact. French dramatists were obviously influenced by the ancients and tried to follow the dramatic rules laid down by Euripides. Their plots might be borrowed from varying sources, but their characters were all given names of figures in classical history, and during the eighteenth century all these tragedies were played in classical costumes.

French comedy took the form of satirical mockery of the modes and habits of contemporary life, and was occasionally accompanied by a ballet. Ballet arrived as a new interest during the second half of the seventeenth century, and schools of dancing quickly turned the ancient chorus into an elegant background of dancing men—and later, women—who appeared between scenes to relieve the boredom of the audiences while the rather cumbersome scenery was being changed.

The encumbering fashions of the late seventeenth century were obviously unsuited to women dancers, and the stiff embroidered garments were discarded in favour of Greek draperies—a daring departure from petticoats. Later these diaphanous draperies were replaced by fantastic pastoral dresses and abbreviated versions of the gowns worn at the French Court. Several of these amusing and unusual *ensembles* have been depicted in the following pages.

These various types of plays were imitated with varying success by Germany and Holland. The German temperament, however, was curiously unsuited to French tragedy, to Spanish drama, or to Italian comedies, and it was not until the end of the eighteenth century that Germany eventually produced noteworthy dramatic works of her own.

Dutch costumes frequently appear in the reproduced drawings. There were, it is true, no particularly well-known or clever Dutch playwrights, and consequently the performances in Holland were mainly imitative productions of foreign plays, yet the influence of Dutch fashions, especially during the seventeenth century, was widespread. The Quaker styles and fashions were considered less fantastic and more serviceable than the Parisian models adopted in England, France, and Germany.

France undoubtedly became the leader of fashion during the eighteenth century, and after that date it will be noticed that feminine costumes in other countries cease to bear an obvious style of their own.

Certain differences in details persist, but the general tendency is to follow more and more the dictates of Paris.

It is my sincere hope that the profuse illustrations in this book will help to give a much clearer idea of details, shape, ornament, and design than could be gathered from a lengthy and possibly boring description in the text. Such items as hairdressing, corseting, hoops, and panniers and the construction of complicated head-dresses need the help of a verbal explanation because in a drawing it is not possible to show clearly and from all angles those things that demand a framework other than the natural form beneath and the more obvious arrangements of certain draperies.

Colour has been suggested in the sixteen colour-plates, but texture and types of materials are dealt with more fully in the text.

The patterns illustrated are not merely casual decorations, but have all been based on contemporary *motifs* of each period, if not actually copied from original designs. The producer would be wise to follow roughly the styles of designs drawn in these pages, as often a too modern pattern may spoil the general effect of an accurately made garment.

Fashions in design are inseparably linked to the history, geography, and architecture of each period, and pastoral simplicity in patterns only occurs when the particular country in which those patterns are produced is luxuriating in a period of peace and plenty. In much the same way we can find the effects of wars reflected in the military styles adopted by women and children of the period in which they occur. The over-decorated furniture and architecture of the time of Louis XV and Louis XVI is again reflected in the exaggerated styles affected in fashions of those years. The gilt and spindly fragility of the Empire buildings and furnishings is inseparably linked to the clinging lines of the Empire gowns, and the pseudo-Greek and classic styles adopted by the ladies of that time.

The most stiff and stilted fashions were more often efforts to imitate some eastern style which appeared amusing to the jaded fancy of a lady of fashion than an outward expression of straight-laced ideals or morals. While the extremest *décolleté* and negligent fashions were more often than not an effort at simplicity after an orgy of over-decorated and ostentatious gaudiness, nevertheless these ' simple ' fashions usually coincided with a period of general slackness—both of manners and person.

Although the illustrations and their descriptions continue into the nineteenth century, this short period is only introduced to round off the possibility of productions recurring some forty years after they first appear. The whole outlook towards the theatre altered so considerably during the early years of the century that to refer to nineteenth-century themes and playwrights would immediately plunge us into a new world altogether. There have been several books written about the theatre of the nineteenth century, and this period cannot be dismissed with a few explanatory notes. It is considerably simpler, then, to close the dramatic side with the finish of the eighteenth century, when historical plays had at last become costume pieces, and the theatre a well-established feature of practically every country—a recognized amusement of not only the Court and the wealthy, but of the people.

One more point of definite value must be stressed—indeed, too much emphasis is impossible—every would-be designer or producer of period plays must remember that exaggeration is a very necessary quality in theatrical costume. Each particular peculiarity of any given date should be singled out and enlarged upon slightly—hoops built a trifle larger so that waists appear smaller; high head-dresses accentuated, frilled cuffs or puffed sleeves frilled or puffed just a little more than seems necessary; colour-contrasts just a little more brilliant and crude than they might have been; embroideries and decorations made larger and more obvious. So many truly lovely costumes have been dwarfed and rendered inconspicuous when they appeared upon the stage by too much attention to small detail and not sufficient concentration on shape and colour—the two most important factors in all theatrical production.

THE THEATRE OF THE SEVENTEENTH CENTURY

OPERATIC drama and the Commedia dell' Arte vied with each other for supremacy throughout the seventeenth century.

The Italian theatre is inseparably linked to the Commedia dell' Arte, and its popularity lasted well into the eighteenth century. These actors, who never learned a part, frequently were only made familiar with the play in which they were to act on the day on which it was produced. They fooled and improvised as much for their own amusement as for the interest of the audience. They were immediately popular, their troupes being welcomed all over Europe.

It is impossible to ignore their very real effect on the stage of the seventeenth century, although their place in the modern theatre has degenerated to the clowning in the Christmas pantomimes.

It was probably due to the very crude and lascivious acting of the Italian women—who, in these plays, always took the part of unfaithful wives—that we find no woman on the stage until the end of the seventeenth century in any country except Italy.

In 1600 Philip III of Spain complained of the behaviour of the actresses in the troupe of Italian players brought over by Alberto Gavasa, and the result was a law prohibiting women from appearing on the stage. Curiously enough, the general feeling in Spain at this time was considerably divided in its reaction to the theatre. At the beginning of the seventeenth century Cervantes and

Lope de Vega were both writing plays which were produced and appeared to be exceedingly popular, especially the work of the·latter. Calderón also had started on the road to dramatic success and popular approval before 1635. Nevertheless Lope de Vega on his death-bed was persuaded to confess to the mortal sin of having written for the stage. So that although this period in Spanish dramatic history is richer by its three most brilliant contributors, their popularity during their lifetime was severely threatened by the disapproval of the Church.

Calderón, who was born in 1601, wrote delightful plays greatly influenced by the romantic works of Cervantes. The last barrier of ecclesiastical condemnation of the theatre must have been broken down when he himself entered the Church. Always religiously inclined, Calderón took holy orders during the later part of his lifetime, but he was not allowed to neglect his dramatic talents in the fulfilment of his religious obligations.

Philip IV insisted that he should remain at Court as a religious adviser as well as a playwright and theatrical manager, and it was under this monarch's approval that the Spanish theatre reached its highest standard.

Philip IV was passionately fond of the theatre, and innumerable dramas appeared under his patronage. He himself was supposed to have written several, quite probably with the assistance of Moreto, a gay and comic dramatist who flourished at that time.

The courtyards, which had previously served as both stage and 'pit,' with the windows of the houses let out as boxes to the grandees, gave place to theatres with built-up stages and a variety of scenic effects in lighting and perspective scenery. Such effects had previously been attempted only by the Italian and French theatres.

Calderón was first summoned to the Court of Philip IV on the death of Lope de Vega, and it is a great misfortune that this very clever playwright was far more interested in his career in the army, and later the Church, than in his undoubted ability to produce delightful romances, for he neither collected nor published his own productions, but left them in the hands of others who afterwards published a number of plays under his name so altered that he himself could not recognize them. It has been said that Calderón turned dreams into flesh and blood, and his themes, even distorted as they are supposed to be, remain charming romantic fragments. He wrote a play for each celebration of the King's birthday, as well as many others. *The Combat of Love, Jealousy,* and *The Lady and her Maid* are all worthy examples of the one hundred and eleven plays which he admits as his own.

With Calderón's death in 1681 the Spanish theatre fell into decline, and since that date very little of merit has been conceived by Spanish dramatists until modern times. The dramatic and theatrical energies of the Italians during this period were wholly taken up with the Commedia dell' Arte on the one hand, and the opera, with its impressive and grandiose scenery and lighting, on the other. Indeed, after 1650 both the French and Italian theatres suffered considerably from the concentrated striving after stage-effects—to the real detriment of the players.

It was not really until the eighteenth century that Italy once more became the home of several very clever dramatists.

Obviously, then, it was left to France to make real progress in dramatic achievement. Corneille (1606–1684), Racine (1639–1699), and Molière (1622–1673) are the three greatest names in seventeenth-century dramatic French history. There are of course many lesser dramatists who followed the lead of these three masters. Unfortunately most of the French dramatists of the seventeenth century concentrated all their efforts on what they considered were the classical rules in dramatic productions. This cult completely obliterated any efforts at contemporary themes, which for our purpose might have been very much more interesting.

Corneille wrote one contemporary comedy, *Le Menteur*, which was taken from one of Lope de Vega's plots. His other works were all heroic tragedies, the most famous of which include *Le Cid* (1636), *Horace, Cinna, Polyeucte* (produced between 1640 and 1643), *Pompée* (1643), *Rodogune* (1644), *Nicomède* (1561), and a heroic comedy *Don Sanche d'Aragon* (1650). When these plays were first produced, the actors were actually dressed in the contemporary fashions, but later during the eighteenth century classical Greek or Roman draperies were invariably worn.

Corneille was extremely popular during his lifetime. Obviously his tragedies satisfied the public demand for rather crude thrills, but Corneille certainly borrowed unblushingly from the works of the Spanish dramatists, though he disguised his characters in the garb of Ancient Rome.

Racine, on the other hand, refused to read the works of other great men and concentrated wholly on the production of pseudo-Greek plays of the accepted form of climactic brevity, viewing things entirely from the psychological aspect. The originality of this viewpoint proved an amazing success, and Racine still ranks as one of the most brilliant playwrights of France. In 1664 he wrote his first tragedy *Thébaïde*, which was succeeded by *Alexandre, Andromaque*, and a comedy, *Les Plaideurs*, in 1668. *Bérénice,*

Bajazet, Mithridate, and *Phèdre* are among the later tragedies. As with Corneille these plays, though of pseudo-classical inspiration, were acted during the remaining years of the seventeenth century in contemporary clothes, and during the eighteenth became established as Greek costume plays.

As true recorders of seventeenth-century manners, Molière, and Regnard in a lesser degree, have left us a variety of intensely amusing and enjoyable light comedies.

With wonderful perception, Molière succeeded in recording the absurdities and pretensions of the professional classes of his time and, with a relentless and damning penetration, proceeded to expose them for the hyper-critical humbugs that they were.

Jean-François Regnard, who wrote his first comedy in 1696, was not so accomplished, nor was his satire so biting. His comedies are considerably lighter than those of Molière but, nevertheless, they are full of action and brightness.

Molière and Regnard were the two outstanding comic playwrights of the seventeenth century, and their popularity has outlived the modes and manners on which they based their comedies. Molière's satirical frivolity and his obvious ridicule of the professional quacks of his time are not only contemporary skits, but charming and amusing situations, whose humour never dates.

His most popular comedies and their approximate dates of production are: *Les Précieuses ridicules* (1659), *L'Ecole des Maris* and *Les Fâcheux* (1661), *Le Misanthrope,* and *Le Médecin malgré lui* (1666), *L'Avare* (1668), *Tartufe* and *Monsieur de Pourceaugnac* (1669), *Le Bourgeois gentilhomme* (1670), *Les Fourberies de Scapin* (1671), *Les Femmes savantes* (1672), and *Le Malade imaginaire* (1673).

Louis XIV of France encouraged dramatic enterprise

and ability even more than Philip IV of Spain had done. He interested himself particularly in ballet, and at a period when only men appeared on the public stage, he made his début at the age of thirteen in *Cassandra*. Later, his interest extended further, and to encourage a greater public interest in acting, singing, and dancing, he issued letters-patent in 1672 which authorized "the faithful and well-beloved Jean-Baptiste Lully to add to the Royal Academy of Music and Dancing, a school suitable to educate pupils as much for dancing as for singing, also to train bands of violins and other instruments."

This encouragement of dramatic art induced several women to take lessons under Lully's instruction, and in 1681 the first professional women dancers appeared on the French stage. Although 1681 was the earliest date in France for professional actresses, noblewomen had taken part in the Court masques for a considerable number of years.

It was at the end of the seventeenth century that the troupes of Italian actors were expelled from Paris for the unforgivable sin of presuming to produce a play entitled *La Fausse Prude*, which was an undisguised attack on the manners of Madame de Maintenon. This temporary banishment—they were recalled in 1716—seemed to excite a further interest in the traditional costumes of the Commedia dell' Arte, and we find many of the Italian figures creeping into the French productions of this period.

Throughout the seventeenth century Germany was making rather futile and colourless efforts to follow both the Spanish and the French theatres, the impossibility of the German temperament to grasp either the ' light, fantastic' touch of the French players, or the romantic, oriental ' blood and thunder' of the Spanish dramatists rendered their attempts both ludicrous and clumsy. While France, England, and Spain were all producing an excellent quality of dramatic art in their separate styles, Italy and Germany floundered behind, probably for want of a capital in which to concentrate their local talents.

Although he is a German himself, Schlegel, in his *Dramatic Literature*, speaks of the " pitiful condition of the theatre in Germany at the end of the seventeenth and the beginning of the eighteenth centuries."

The Germans apparently contented themselves with the production of ' wretched imitations ' after the worst type of French pastoral plays, which were popular for no other reason than that they were the only dramatic efforts to be found in seventeenth-century Germany.

It was not until the second half of the eighteenth century that Lessing, Goethe, and Schiller eventually rescued the German theatre from mediocre insipidity.

SEVENTEENTH-CENTURY DRESS

THE clothes worn during the seventeenth century in different countries present striking differences, even more noticeable than those of the preceding centuries.

Indeed, there seems to be no other period in the history of costume like that of the years from 1620 to 1660, when nations clung so tenaciously to their accepted styles of dress, refusing to be influenced by the Court fashions.

France made the most marked strides in breaking away from the stiff old styles of farthingales and bombasted and padded limbs, stiff ruffles, and tight waists. Indeed, the French fashions were entirely revolutionary during the 'twenties. A sudden abandonment of all the established stiffness and bombast set in, and the new styles, that must have shocked the straight-laced veteran, called for softly curling tresses, high waists, full loose skirts, and dainty ribbons and lace. Men's fashions were equally sudden in their changes. Fashion had, with one mighty stroke, pricked the bubble of bombast and in the process had revealed the endless possibilities of folds and draperies.

By about 1625 not one item of French apparel resembled the fashion of ten years before. The silhouette, both male and female, had undergone a complete change. Abraham Bosse has left us a very comprehensive collection of prints of these times which show the excesses and absurdities which quickly followed the introduction of informality in clothing.

Frizzed and curled locks tied with bows of ribbon in unexpected places and gigantic hats with small crowns and cart-wheel brims weighed down with ostrich feathers

SPANISH   DUTCH   FRENCH
(1630)
Fig. 1

replaced the close-cropped heads with their high-crowned hats of a decade ago. Materials, from being heavy, stiff, and unresisting, were now soft and diaphanous in texture. The sausage-like distension of the breeches and sleeves collapsed limply into a froth of lace and ribbon. The breeches of the 'twenties were split from knee to mid-

FRENCH   DUTCH   SPANISH

(1630)

Fig. 2

thigh and contrasting linings hung out over the garter at the side. The new coats or doublets were cut short to the waist and finished with a row of flaps. Sometimes, indeed, the jacket was little more than an apology for a coat and consisted of a series of ribbons attached at intervals and showing a contrasting lining. The waist-line was high and usually ornamented by a series of rosettes of ribbon at intervals of two or three inches. Stiffened lace collars, curved into an arc from shoulder to shoulder, framed the face, and later, when the hair became even longer, fell back over the shoulders.

The Frenchwoman cast aside her farthingale and stomacher, and with an almost audible sigh of relief adopted a higher waist-line, softly falling skirts, and a multitude of ribbons and lace in place of starch, whalebone, and gems.

The neatly piled head-dresses—cruelly drawn away from the face—were replaced by impudent curls that clustered over each ear, and the forehead, which for so many years had remained bare, could now be veiled with a row of curls or a fringe. Gone were the gem-studded wigs, and now the only decoration for the hair was bunches of ribbon or a flower.

Finely worked lace, silken ribbons, and strings of pearls, pastel shades, and dainty-patterned materials of cobweb consistency now graced the halls of France.

France, however, remained for several years the only addict to her own styles. The stiffness that characterized Queen Elizabeth's time was general throughout Western Europe, and this, coupled with the lasting quality of the heavy, well-made materials and the vast quantities of expensive ornaments that had been lavished on suits and gowns during the sixteenth century, helped to keep the creaseless, doll-like fashions of a past age in sharp contrast to the softer and more becoming styles of the French Court.

By 1630, however, we find that these styles are accepted by most of the Courts in Western Europe, with the exception of Spain and Portugal—but this applies to the Courts alone, and that with certain reservations.

DUTCH (1615)
Fig. 3

Spain and Portugal clung with tenacious adherence to the fashions of the sixteenth century. Even as late as the 'sixties farthingales were still to be found in the Spanish Courts. Samuel Pepys writes of the absurd farthingales worn by the Portuguese ladies who arrived in the Queen's train in 1662. Although these exaggerated court-fashions are more reminiscent of the hooped skirts of the eighteenth century in shape, they were nevertheless the exaggerated outcome of the original suggestion in the Spanish vertingale of the late sixteenth century.

Spanish fashions for ladies altered hardly at all for a period of eighty years. Clothes worn in 1560 could apparently be easily worn as late as 1640 with little or no alteration.

SPANISH (1622)

Fig. 4

There was a little more acknowledgment of the prevailing fashions in men's attire, but even here the bombasted breeches and slashed sleeves, padded shoulders and hanging sleeves, and a preference for short hair lasted well into the 'thirties.

Dutch fashions during the first quarter of the century adopted and adapted the tight, boned stomachers, pinched waists, padded hips, full skirts, lace bonnets, ruffles, and stiff collars, which became the foundation of their so-called national costume. Even in these ultra-civilized days, there are still to be found a few adherents to these styles in various parts of Holland.

The farthingale itself was abandoned in every country except Spain and Portugal during the 'twenties, but those who still clung to the established fashion for hips obtained the effect with the assistance of a horseshoe-shaped roll of horse-hair which was tied round the waist beneath the petticoats.

Dutch ladies kept to the old style of high-crowned black hat, which was more often than not worn over a close-fitting lace cap. They were still wearing these in the 1660's in preference to the large, soft-brimmed hats favoured by the majority of countries at that date. After a tentative experiment in French modes, Holland broke away and introduced several new and very charming styles entirely of her own design.

Chief among these Dutch modes was that for becoming little caps and hats, close-fitting and usually made of lace or fine lawn. This

DUTCH (1620)
Fig. 5

was at a period when France had abandoned any form of head-dress, and all the attention that had previously been lavished upon hats and caps was now concentrated on curling and arranging the hair becomingly round the face. Should my lady wish to pro-

DUTCH (1627)
Fig. 6

tect her head from the inclement weather, a scarf or hood was deemed less likely to disturb her carefully arranged coiffure than a hat. And if perchance the sun was too likely to freckle or sunburn or dazzle the eyes, a little mask

FRENCH (1626)
Fig. 7

was carried to afford the face the necessary protection. The fear of the effects of sun on the skin was so great during the period 1630–1650 that veils laid over the hair and reaching to the shoulders were frequently worn in the summer.

French fashions in hairdressing continued to take the lead until the close of the century, and the styles were both many and varied.

By 1640 the feminine silhouette had again changed,

ITALIAN (1623)
Fig. 8

and French and Dutch fashions competed for an established popularity in other countries.

In France the waist-line dropped to normal, the huge puffed sleeves gave place to a slightly less exaggerated form of the earlier fashion. The deep lace collar was

GERMAN (1625)
Fig. 9

SPANISH (1640)
Fig. 10

DUTCH (1645)

Fig. 11

brought to the front of the bodice and formed a V-neck.
The overskirt was bunched and folded back. It was
often tied with ribbons, and revealed a long laced apron
probably worn over a flowered petticoat.

The Dutch fashions were considerably less decorative.
Lace was not so popular, and deep linen collars from

the throat to well over the shoulders covered a tight-fitting, short-waisted bodice. Sleeves were usually worn fitting the arm and terminating in a deep linen cuff. The style for folding back the overskirt, however, was generally popular, but plain materials decorated with bands of some contrasting colours were more general in Holland than the daintily flowered fabrics of France.

A tightly laced corset had once more become a necessity for the fashionable Frenchwoman. The waist-line and corset of the seventeenth century were perpetually changing.

The long-boned stomachers of the early seventeenth century and the short, high-waisted gowns which required no corset have already been mentioned, but each of these styles was accompanied by an entirely different type of skirt. From 1650 to 1700 the skirts remained fundamentally the same, but the corset varied considerably with each new decade. A full, gathered skirt was worn over a contrasting petticoat, the overskirt being split up the front and folded back, or bunched up in a variety of styles which followed not so much the dictates of fashion as the whims and inclinations of the owners. The width and length of these gowns varied slightly with the years. At times they barely touched the ground, and a few years later they swept in a pointed train behind. These styles, however, were mere local idiosyncrasies : for utilitarian purposes the shorter skirt was always a favourite—and for more formal occasions the train gave a stately and regal appearance.

It was during the 'forties that Frenchwomen once more began to tight-lace themselves, and by 1650 a small waist was an absolute necessity to the well-dressed lady.

The bodices of their gowns were cut to finish at the normal waist-line at the back, but extended to a slightly curved or pointed U shape in front. The line from armpit to waist definitely curved inward and was not straight as all the earlier corsets had been.

Gradually the length of the V in the front was exaggerated and stiffened until the 'sixties, when a very peculiar silhouette was the ultimate result. This quaint stiffness

SPANISH (1659)
Fig. 12

FRENCH   SPANISH   DUTCH

(1660)

Fig. 13

DUTCH (1660)
Fig. 14

DUTCH (1665)
Fig. 15

was accentuated by the deep lace collars which were worn
tightly fitting over the shoulder, often reaching nearly to
the elbow. These collars were either high to the throat
or worn right off the shoulder—a new style in daring
revelation. Sleeves remained full and fluffy until the

DUTCH (1666)
Fig. 16

'seventies, when a cuff or gathered edge replaced the
'puff' so popular in previous years. The tight, stiff, long,
pointed bodice with its sharp little curve over the hips
was succeeded in the 'seventies by an even more wooden
affair which encased the body from armpit to just below
the waist in an unrelenting cylinder forcing the breasts
upward, so that a too revealing curve had to be decorously
covered with a soft swathing of lace or net. These stiff and

DUTCH (1675)
Fig. 17

uncomfortable stays were replaced during the closing years
of the century by corsets giving the effect of armour.
The fashions for pseudo-classical dress had made a loose-
sleeved low-necked shift the popular attire for the lady in
the privacy of her home, and these embroidered corslets

worn over the shift served to give a severe finish to a gown which might otherwise appear too much like a *négligée*: Gems of all kinds were stitched on to the gowns of the wealthy, and a curious stiffness resulted. Heavy gold and silver fringes and scroll-work embroideries helped to foster this fashion.

The stiff, high corset was worn for more formal occasions well into the eighteenth century, but the classical style for draperies had done much to introduce freedom into domestic wear.

During the 'forties the deflated effect disappeared from men's clothes, and after a few years' experimental adjustment of knee-breeches with an assortment of coats of

FRENCH (1685)
Fig. 18

varying lengths, an entirely new fashion made its appearance. This consisted of a short coat or jacket barely reaching to the waist, and full loose breeches of knee-length

FRENCH (1685)
Fig. 19

PORTUGUESE (1688)
Fig. 20

DUTCH (1660 AND 1665)
Fig. 21

similar to very full ' shorts.' The extreme brevity of these
garments was made up for by the superabundance of decoration which they received. An absolute mania for ribbon
and lace developed during the late 'forties and continued
to be an outstanding item of decoration for masculine
garments until the end of the century. Hundreds of yards
of ribbon must have gone to the making of some of these
suits, and the more ornate and absurdly over-burdened

DUTCH (1666)

Fig. 22

with ornaments they became, the more popular was this fashion.

Loops of ribbon were arranged all round the waist of the breeches—often all round the hems. Bunches were sewn nonchalantly down the sides, or arranged in tiers from hips to knee—or even, in more excessive cases, sewn on to flaps that hung from the waist to just below the hem of the breeches. Bows appeared on the shoulders, at the elbows, on garters, sword-belt, hats, in the hair, and on the toes of shoes. In fact, there was no limit to the places where ribbons might be grouped.

This fashion, absurd though it was, spread quickly to other countries, and it is from Holland that we find records of the most exaggerated styles worn during the 'fifties and 'sixties.

The man of the seventeenth century was undeniably the wearer of fine feathers, and the ' mere female ' far less over-dressed and excessively decorated. Ribbons, lace, feathers, and curly coiffures—usually feminine prerogatives —all became for a short time more important to the man

FRENCH (1660)

Fig. 23

than the actual cut of his clothes, for indeed with these lavishly over-ornamented garments little if anything could be seen of the shape beneath. Any mistake that the tailor made could be easily covered up by an aptly placed bunch of ribbon or frill of lace.

With the approach of the 'sixties, even the absurdly full and festooned petticoat breeches failed to please the passion for decoration of their French wearers, and a new garment was evolved with a full, gathered leg below the knee, finished with a deep frill of lace or ribbon loops, and over this a skirt full and decorated that reached almost to the knee. What little leg remained visible beneath these garments was usually adorned by the drooping boot-hose or stocking-tops laced and embroidered and falling almost over the beribboned shoe itself. (Fig. 23.)

A new long-coat just made its appearance during the late 'sixties, and probably because of its violent contrast to former styles, it quickly became universally popular. At first it was a long, loose coat, with short sleeves, split twelve inches or so up the back, and often decorated with buttons. This was worn over the still full and over-decorated breeches. By about 1670 the coat was waisted and could be worn buttoned right down the front. Bunches of ribbon decorated the shoulders, and turned-back cuffs the sleeves. These cuffs might begin at the elbow or several inches down the forearm. Breeches remained full and frilled. At the close of the 'seventies more decoration was attained by the addition of a contrasting long waist-coat—the coat left undone to show off this new garment to its full advantage. Lace and silk-embroidered sashes were quite often tied round the waist over the coat. The pockets, cuffs, and sleeves were usually decorated, and the skirts of the coat, now considerably fuller, were split up the sides as well as the back to permit the wearing of a sword and to supply yet another excuse for border decoration.

Soon after 1680 the full breeches vanished and were replaced by fairly tight-fitting knee-breeches worn under the stocking. The latter were now gartered above the knee and the attention was entirely devoted to the decora-tion of the coat and waistcoat. The split sides were quite often pleated and finished with a button. Cuffs continued to grow in size till the end of the century, when they became large, flapping, and ungainly pieces of material from elbow to wrist. Waistcoats were sometimes sleeved with long, tight sleeves showing several inches below the cuff and sometimes loose and terminating only a few inches below—just long enough to show a contrasting band of material.

Bunches of ribbon were still very popular in the closing

FRENCH (1665)
Fig. 24

DUTCH (1680)
Fig. 25

DUTCH (1680)
Fig. 26

ITALIAN (1683)
Fig. 27

DANISH (1688)
Fig. 28

GERMAN (1683)
Fig. 29

years of the century, being worn on the shoulders, cuffs, and sword-belt.

A fashion for gigantic muffs fastened to the sash by a large ring was vastly indulged by the gallants of the time.

With their feathered hats, huge wigs, muffs, full-skirted

FRENCH (1694)
Fig. 30

coats, cloaks, and high-heeled shoes, they must have been every bit as over-dressed and effeminate as their predecessors of the 'sixties; although the whole style had undergone a change, nothing indeed remained of the earlier styles and fashions, except the wig, which had been exaggerated out of all recognition.

The early wigs had come into fashion first in France, when Louis XIV began to lose his hair, and the fashion demanded that every man must display a fine head of hair. He quickly overcame his natural deficiency in the particular and ordered periwigs of real hair of sumptuous thickness and curls to make up, probably, for several previous years when his own had failed to please. Once wig-makers had discovered the marvels they could create and the substantial fortunes they could accumulate, nothing stopped their fantastic adventures, until the wigs became unwieldy and unmanageable and hats an absurdity.

Hairdressing has always been very much influenced by the shapes and styles of dresses worn at a particular period. One can see this during the seventeenth century when each country followed its own styles of dress. For instance, in France, during the early years of the century, when bombast and farthingales were worn, women's hair was piled and puffed on top of the head and held out with frames, or else a wig was worn, the general effect being puffed and unnatural. When the French gowns of the 'twenties became soft and fell once more in folds, the hair was dressed with equal softness and hung pleasantly and unpretentiously to the lobe of the ear or even to the shoulders. Later, during the 'forties and 'fifties, as the dresses began to assume a double skirt or panniered effect, the hair was more obviously parted in the middle and draped half up and half down, usually with long curls in the front and a plait or roll behind. During the 'seventies, when the overskirt had frankly taken on a bustle effect behind, the hair was dressed in a ' boss,' or cluster of curls at the back (Fig. 32). As the sides of the dress became fuller and more bunched up, the hair was puffed at the sides with curls drawn from behind resting on the shoulders (Fig. 32). With the fashion of the 'eighties and 'nineties — a stiffened skirt and softly draped panniers—hairdressing became an interesting and amusing combination of stiffness and informality

FRENCH (1629)
Fig. 31

(1670)

(1680)

(1690)

(1693)

Fig. 32

with its carefully arranged curls, each with a name and place, and the absurdly ornate pinner head-dresses, decorated with frontally arranged ribbons and gems in much the same way as the gowns themselves.

Spain, in contrast, clung to her stiffly padded skirts and farthingales and retained the old, high-piled, puffed, and padded hairdressing of the late sixteenth century well into the 'forties. When the extremely full hooped skirts of the 'fifties superseded the less exaggerated fashion, the hair became a miniature replica of the absurd skirts themselves, and was curled and puffed, plaited and tied with

SPANISH (1629)   SWEDISH (1629)

Fig. 33

bows until it stood away from the head to a ridiculously unnatural shape (Fig. 34).

Dutch and German styles followed two modes—both that of France and their own adaptation of the older fashion. Thus throughout the century we find a certain percentage of women wearing the scraped-back hair and tight-fitting bonnets and caps, and those of more frivolous inclinations following the more 'undressed' fashions of the French Court.

SPANISH (1652)
Fig. 34

Men's modes of hairdressing also followed the silhouette to a great extent.

Where the ruffle was worn, the hair had of necessity to be worn short, but with the wide, wing-like collars of the 'twenties and 'thirties the hair underwent a variety of extraordinary changes. The loose, slightly bedraggled effect of the deflated garments with their trimmings of ribbon and still puffy sleeves were almost exactly imitated by the hairdressing of the French fops and gallants of the time. The hair was frizzed and puffed around the face and trailed off into what were then called ' love-locks '—strands, or curls of hair, tied at the extreme ends with bows of ribbon and arranged to fall nonchalantly over the shoulders. In the extremest addicts to the follies of fashion the head rather resembled the matted untidiness of the head of a child's doll that has lain unattended for many years. However, as the high-waisted doublets assumed more normal proportions, and the floppy breeches were replaced by a more closely fitting leg-covering, the hair also assumed a more normal aspect and was worn brushed into fairly neat curls usually reaching just over the shoulders to rest on the beautifully worked lace-collars that had superseded the high curved ones of the 'twenties and 'thirties. Later, as the fashions once more became exaggerated, full-skirted, and absurdly over-ornamented, the periwig was the fashionable imitation of the frilled and flounced silhouette. With its masses of curls often reaching half-way down the back there is an undeniable resemblance to the many-tiered coat and petticoat-breeches and boot-hose that were the accepted form of dress during the 'sixties, and any form of hairdressing of smaller proportions would no doubt have rendered the head ridiculously small in contrast to the over-ornamented body beneath.

As coats changed into the long full-skirted shape that was to be so popular for a century or more, the periwigs assumed even larger and more incongruous proportions and were eventually divided into three separate masses of curls—as indeed the skirts of the coat were divided to give

A (1625)   B (1645) C (1665)   D (1685)

Fig. 35

greater freedom and more accessibility to the sword and pockets beneath.

Masculine footwear worn in the seventeenth century was both amusing and various. Here again, French fashions favoured the exaggerated styles that were not adopted by the more sober-minded countries.

During the first twenty years of the century the shoe was usually low-cut at the sides, with a square toe and a heel an inch or two in height, the instep being adorned by a large bow or rosette or even a bunch of lace decorated with beads and gems. The curious fashion for bucket-top boots came into being during the 'twenties and remained a favourite absurdity for some twenty years. Not content with the width at the top of these boots, huge butterfly tabs adorned the instep and held the spurs in place. Boot-hose were worn inside. These were long stockings with the tops made about the same width as the tops of the boots. Embroidered and decorated, they hung down over the turned-back boot-tops. Another form of decoration was the ' stocking-tops,' or merely embroidered pieces to give the appearance of the boot-hose without fulfilling the latter's dual purpose of saving friction on the hose beneath as well as being ornamental.

In France these boots assumed absurd proportions—so ungainly they became, indeed, that it was with the greatest difficulty that the ' gallants ' or cavaliers could successfully straddle along.

Except for riding, the boot vanished during the 'sixties, and shoes once more became the vogue. This time, however, the toe was considerably elongated, being to all appearances at least an inch or so longer than the foot. The toe was square and flattened and reached up to an elongated tongue or flap several inches above the ankle.

A

(1630)

B

(1640)

C

(1655)

D

(1670)

Fig. 36

These flaps were invariably decorated with a buckle, which, in its turn, was decorated with gems or paste. The tongue or flap could be cut in a variety of shapes, and, more often than not, it was lined with a contrasting material or leather. Heels were high, absurdly so in some cases, and quite frequently square in shape. Often when the tongue was lined, the heel also was of a contrasting colour, usually scarlet.

Women's shoes were fragile and inconsequent affairs of embroidered silk, satin, or velvet. Their durability and utility were practically negligible.

The materials employed in the making of garments were numerous. In the early years of the seventeenth century velvets and plush, satins and silks of a stiff nature were mostly used; the fashion for damasks and heavy materials richly embroidered or interwoven with gold and silver thread only lasted in France until about 1615. But in Spain and Italy these richly decorated and stiffened fabrics were used considerably until the middle of the century.

About 1620 the new softness of style in French gowns and skirts required a much softer and more flimsy material to carry out the deflated idea which was so fashionable after the abandonment of the bombast and farthingale. Spotted and flowered lawn figured largely in the wardrobe of the fashionable lady, while soft pastel-coloured silks and linens were frequently used for men's suits.

A few years later taffetas became universally popular, and a softer type of velvet than had previously been used was often employed in men's garments. Woven silk hose were quite a common extravagance for the first fifteen or twenty years of the century. This was richly em-

DUTCH (1690)
Fig. 37

broidered with a variety of coloured silks. Later, when the boot-hose and stocking-tops were the fashionable extravagance, these beautifully embroidered pieces of linen supplanted the more colourful leg-wear of earlier years.

It is impossible to think of the seventeenth century without immediately visualizing lace and ribbons, and from about 1640 to 1670 it was quite possible to make an entire gown or suit with these two flimsy substances and the assistance of a silk lining.

The Dutch fashions were considerably heavier in effect than the frothy effervescence of the French frills and furbelows, and dyed linen, holland, and fustian, or woollen cloth, were more often used in the making of clothes than silks, taffetas, and laces. By reason of the fullness of the fashions it was impossible to employ heavy materials, as their weights and bulk would destroy the graceful effect of soft folds which were so typical of the mid-seventeenth century.

The full petticoat-breeches worn by the men relied again for their effect on the brief, vertical folds from waist to knee, and fullness was attained not by a stiffly hanging material, which would have stood out too widely from the waist, but by the lavish ornamentation at the edges of a tightly gathered fine or medium weight fabric. It was not until the 'seventies that heavier woven and thickly embroidered stuffs were once more employed.

As long as tailoring was not a real requisite for fashionable dressing, soft, unstiffened materials were of more importance for their decorative quality of drapery. Directly the long coat with fitted shoulders and waisted back appeared in the late 'sixties the demand for substance and ' dressing ' was immediately required in fabrics.

VENETIAN (1690)
Fig. 38

Brocades and richly embroidered silks and velvets were employed mostly for formal wear. Woollens and fustians replaced the linens of a few years earlier.

Calico was still something of a novelty and, because of the difficulties of importation, it became extremely desirable. Block-printed motifs and hand-painted flowers were both used extensively as a method of decoration. Curiously enough, as the men's fashions in fabrics gradually stiffened and became more solid, women also adopted the less fragile materials, and instead of employing limp lace and the softest of embroideries or ribbons, they concentrated their energies on making gold and silver lace, stiff and solid in texture, and decorated their gowns with heavy fringe and tassels, gems and precious stones adding richness to the new formality.

Petticoats, quilted from hem to knee, helped to support the fuller skirts of the 'eighties. Oriental silks of rich thick texture 'crackled' and 'swished' over the hooped supports of the 'nineties. Flanders lace and point lace were both lavishly used on underwear and *négligée*.

Though floral designs were still fashionable until the 'nineties, stripes and flowers embroidered between stripes were more successful in the scheme of stiffness, embroideries were often copied from designs more suited to metal-work than fabrics, and scrolls, loops, and other shapes adapted from classical architecture decorated the petticoat and corsage of the elegant Frenchwoman of the late 'nineties.

THE THEATRE OF THE EIGHTEENTH CENTURY

THE production of an opera in eighteenth - century Italy necessitated almost as much lavish expenditure and probably almost as much work as that of a super-Hollywood film of to-day. The scenic effects were positively breath-taking in their splendour and size, and experiments in lighting and transformation scenes involved endless constructional work, made more difficult by the rather clumsy and inadequate machinery of the time.

Contemporary writers were rich in their praise of the clever illusions that were carried out without hitches. Coloured lights were obtained by the use of gigantic bottles of coloured fluids, similar to the bottles that used to adorn the windows of every chemist's shop. The cleverest artists of the time devoted themselves to the intricacies of furthering the architectural and scenic effects and illusions, and drawings of these vast opera-houses give one an impression of space and splendour certainly never achieved in the English theatre of the twentieth century.

While so much thought and energy were put into the actual stage and background for the players, the players themselves were completely dwarfed by their surroundings. The theatre indeed appeared to be of far greater interest as a spectacle in itself than as a setting for the tiny figures who danced and sang behind the footlights. It was in all probability due to this splendid scenery that practically no collected sets of costumes existed. Only the leading artists were furnished with ' suitable ' apparel for their parts and this was often as over-decorated and rococo as the surroundings. The smaller parts and choruses were played in almost any property clothes in much the same way that a collection of children to-day, in playing charades or theatricals, will don any disguise rather than appear as they are.

The magnificence of the Italian opera-houses had reached a height never previously dreamed of in the wildest flights of theatrical fancy. And no other European country could attempt to come near them in their glistening splendour. But it remains a curious fact that, from the point of view of historical accuracy, the costumes were merely bizarre and ridiculous for at least the first half of the eighteenth century.

Although practically all dramatic authors of this time specialized in historic and oriental themes, the idea of costume was definitely not considered. In fact, any departure from the approved though utterly unauthentic style of dressing all the male actors in pseudo-Roman armour of peculiar design, and encouraging the actresses to wear the most exaggerated and fantastic versions of the latest fashions, met with immediate disapproval.

It was in France that a reform of costume eventually took place.

In 1753 Mme Favart appeared on the stage as a villager. Her hair was in plaits ; she wore a rough serge gown ; and she had bare arms and legs and her feet were in sabots. This departure from the accepted and almost traditional operatic costume caused a lot of harsh criticism. It was considered a poor style which served to cheapen dramatic art.

Voltaire's *l'Orphelin de la Chine* was played in Chinese costume as early as 1755, and Chaussée's *l'Amour Castillan* was played at about the same time in Spanish costume.

FRENCH (1730)
Fig 39

It was probably very unreal but, none the less, it was an attempt that caused considerable surprise, and was considered a daring departure which met with little approval.

The heroine in Voltaire's *Mérope* appeared in a brocade gown with panniers. Her hair was powdered, and she had patches on her face, and this appearance was not considered either humorous or out of place.

In fact a contemporary theatrical authority writes in 1755 that "historical exactitude is impossible and fatal to dramatic art." So a sort of half-reform was arrived at which still gave the player considerable scope for his or her fancy in dress. It is an amusing fact that when *Brutus* was played in 1768, the actors were in a Greek temple and the soldiers dressed in Mexican style with guns and bayonets.

Many arrangements of costume that were equally silly and out of place occurred from time to time throughout the century.

Ballet costume appeared in a more or less accepted style of its own in about 1720, the ladies of the ballet wearing huge hooped skirts festooned with garlands of roses and bows of ribbon. The shoes had a small heel, and the skirts were about ten or twelve inches from the ground. The male ballet performers were still satisfied with the pseudo-classic taste for armour resulting in a sort of abbreviated ballet skirt, and with a gigantic feathered helmet on the head. During the 'thirties the pastoral influence suggested the possibilities of a full-skirted coat and knee-breeches, and this comparatively simple conversion of everyday wear became almost as popular as the earlier styles.

Although Italian opera had reached such a very high standard of scenic perfection during the last years of the seventeenth century, and the early years of the eighteenth, the Parisian theatre was still something of a novelty, and Paris only boasted three proper theatres : L'Académie Royal, the Comédie Française, and a room in the Hôtel de Bourgogne where first Molière and later the Italian comedians played.

Lully had tried to start an open-air theatre near the Luxembourg gardens. It was not, however, a successful enterprise, although apparently it had been lavishly fitted out with the latest mechanical devices, as well as an orchestra and ballet.

Lully and Molière had done much to perfect and improve theatrical conditions, and after their deaths the French theatre seems to have floundered somewhat on the rocks of the absurd convention which demanded splendour without taste or intelligence.

It was probably due to Beaumarchais' efforts in the second half of the century that both scenery and costumes were given a little more thought, and a certain connexion with the themes of the productions. Beaumarchais was addicted to exact scenery, and he obviously did not feel that a magnificent Gothic setting or a Greek temple was an appropriate background to his *Barber of Seville*.

Although there were so few real theatres in Paris during the early years of the century, there were numerous small private theatres. Indeed, practically all the wealthy aristocracy had converted rooms in their mansions specially for the production of theatrical enterprises.

The whole of France had become what we should probably term ' theatre-conscious ' by about the middle of the century. Under the auspicious encouragement of Marie Antoinette the theatre became a popular diversion.

Spain, which, during the seventeenth century, had produced such a wealth of exciting, romantic, and adventure-

FRENCH (1770)
Fig. 40

some themes for drama, had now fallen behind or was, at the best, a source from which French or Italian writers could draw their plots. Italy was still absorbed in her magnificent and spectacular experiments in stage-effects, and dramatic authors sprang up like mushrooms to furnish her wonderful theatres with adequately inspiring operas and plays. Either poetic genius seemed to be easier to foster than dramatic prose, or else it met with more encouragement. So we find that the majority of Italian playwrights of the eighteenth century limited their adventures to the production of opera—or operetta.

One of the earliest of these poetic geniuses of the eighteenth century was Pietro Metastasio, an Italian born in Rome in 1698. Although brought up to study law, he discovered that lyrical poetry ran insistently through his mind, and interfered considerably with his scholastic efforts. He eventually wrote an operetta, *Gli Orti Esperidi*, admirably set to music of his own composition, but still imagining that this was a waste of time, he allowed it to be produced only on the understanding that he should remain anonymous.

It was acted in Naples with splendid decorations and was an immediate and outstanding success. Its authorship was eventually discovered by the prima donna Marianna Bulgarini, who had played Venus, the lead in this production. Her unexpected patronage and admiration caused him to abandon his law-training and devote himself entirely to dramatic writing and music. So spontaneous was this artist that he admitted to never writing lyrical poetry without imagining the musical accompaniments. In 1724 he wrote *Didone abbandonata* and *Siroe*. His drama of *Cato* was acted in 1727, and he was elected Court Poet of Vienna in 1730. After that date he wrote only a few theatrical works, including *Alessandro nell' Indie* and *Artaserse*.

Although Metastasio was admittedly an inspired composer of light operatic work during the early years of the eighteenth century, it is to Goldoni that the honours must be paid as a reformer of Italian comedy. Goldoni, born in 1707, discovered at an early age his theatrical inclinations, and, after joining a troupe of Italian comedians, he decided that their inconsequent improvisation and forced situations could be considerably improved by the introduction of a plot founded on natural incidents and definite parts learnt by heart. To this end he devoted himself, and with so great a success that an entirely new type of comic theatre was established in Italy, and the old order of actors who preferred not to memorize their parts, but to exaggerate and buffoon, unhampered by these new restrictions, were forced to limit their activities generally to the provinces of their own and other countries where strolling players were still welcomed. Goldoni, like so many of his predecessors, looked for his early inspirations among the old dramas of *Griselda* and *Don Giovanni*. Afterwards he followed the example of Molière ; *Donna di Garbo* and *The Daughter of the Lacemaker* were both written from truly contemporary life, and he found in the Venetian modes and manners of the mid-eighteenth century an inexhaustible supply of themes which his ready wit and dramatic talents turned into a brilliant record of his time. He was extraordinarily prolific in his writings, and, at one time he succeeded in completing sixteen comedies between seasons. Of these, *The Pernicious Ladies*, *La Pamela*, *The Prudent Lady*, and *The Gossipings* were the most popular. Goldoni, encouraged by his success in Italy, went to Paris in 1761, in an effort to reform the Italian comedians still so popular in France. However, they did not welcome the prospect of having to learn their parts, and Goldoni's enterprise was not immediately successful. Nevertheless, he did produce one brilliant comedy in Paris, *Le Bourru Bienfaisant*, which Voltaire praises as the most brilliant French farce since Molière.

Alfieri (1749–1803) was another Italian playwright of undoubted talent, but with a horror of being influenced by the works of other dramatists. He refused to read any of the works of his predecessors for fear of imitating their style or copying their plots. Most of his dramatic works are founded on the lives of Biblical or historical figures. *Mirra* is considered his most successful tragedy out of fourteen which include: *Maria Stuarda*, *Rosmunda*, *Octavia*, *Filippo*, *Antigone*, *Polinice*, *Virginia*, *Bruto*, and *Agide*. All these tragedies were written and produced before the end of the 'eighties, and none of them was founded on contemporary eighteenth-century life. A highly strung and easily depressed temperament resulted in Alfieri's complete breakdown when confronted with the arduous and rather soul-shattering job of correcting proofs of his works for publication, and during the last twenty years of his life he produced nothing.

Monti, who has since been acknowledged as the greatest Italian poet since the golden days of poetry, was born in 1754 and died in 1826. His *Aristodemo* was first acted in Rome in 1787 and was successfully accompanied by the usual eighteenth-century embellishments. He specialized in bloodthirsty and highly imaginative rhapsodies, undoubtedly influenced by the old Spanish writers. The last outstanding efforts in Italian eighteenth-century drama were those of Ugo Foscolo. In 1797, at the early age of nineteen, he produced a drama *Thyestes*, written with some skill but rather over-influenced by the works of Alfieri. His only other theatrical work was *Ajax*, produced in 1813, which was singularly heavy and not particularly successful.

Italian opera was considered the most exquisite of all dramatic entertainments and was encouraged and welcomed throughout Europe.

In France a variety of playwrights made their appearance during the century. Regnard was still a popular writer of light comedy when the century opened. His *Les Folies amoureuses* and *Le Légataire universel* were both produced before 1708. Le Sage (1668–1747) specialized in light comedies and Spanish romances. *Crispin rival de son maître* (1707), *Turcaret* (1709), and *l'Histoire de Gil Blas* (1715) were all successful productions founded on contemporary French manners and customs.

Voltaire was one of the most successful French dramatic writers of the eighteenth century. His works are full of the spirited vivacity of the old Spanish writers, and his historical and classic romances gave the splendour-loving public all that they could possibly demand in the way of colourful drama and heart-rending tragedy. His first work was the tragedy of *Œdipe*, produced in 1718. He found time between the writings of his various histories to produce several outstandingly successful tragedies, including *Brutus* (1730), *Zaïre* (1732), *La Mort de César* (1735), *Algire* (1736), *Mahomet* (1741), *Mérope* (1743), *l'Orphelin de la Chine* (1755), and *Tancrède* (1760).

Beaumarchais distinguished himself in 1775 by writing *Le Barbier de Séville* and *Le Mariage de Figaro* in 1784, both brilliant and sparkling comedies which have earned him a theatrical reputation of merit. He also wrote three dramas which were not anything like as successful—*Eugénie* (1767), *Les Deux Amis* (1770), and *La Mère coupable* (1791).

There were numerous French writers of the eighteenth century who attempted to write satirical comedies in the Molière tradition—light or frivolous commentaries on the modes and manners of an age of insincerity and intrigue. Among these Legrand, Marivaux, Favart, Destouches, Dancourt, Anseaume, and Florian have all left us several works which are typical of their time.

Light comedies were encouraged in France probably as an antidote to heavy melodrama, and many of these pieces were adapted for the Italian stage, as indeed the farcical Italian comedies were translated for the French theatre.

For nearly a century France and Italy had supplied the Continent with all the dramatic efforts of merit, when at long last Germany produced, in Lessing, a dramatic author filled with a zest to improve the insipid productions that were then characteristic of Germany. Curiously enough, Germany boasted several extremely good actors at this period, and as Lessing aptly expresses it : " We have actors but no dramatic art—if, in times gone by, such an art existed, we no longer possess it, it is lost and has to be invented anew." And he set himself the task of inventing it anew. It was Lessing undoubtedly who put in all the spade-work of breaking down the vogue for old, adapted, and poorly produced French plays, and pointed to Shakespeare as the real leader of the cultivated theatre.

In 1767 he successfully produced a true comedy of ' refined class ' called *Minna von Barnhelm* which was an immediate success in Germany and established his earlier works as something in the nature of German classics. *Emilia Galotti* (1772) and *Nathan der Weise* (1779) were both welcomed with great applause.

Schiller established himself as yet another dramatic author of considerable merit with *The Robbers*, produced in 1782. His themes were rather grotesque, and certainly not refined, but they undoubtedly met with the appreciation of his audiences. It is interesting to find that here in Germany the ' costume ' period had not yet arrived. When *The Robbers* was produced, Dalberg, the producer, decided that modern costumes might appear absurd in the fantastic setting of the play—and the playbills stated that the piece was supposed to have taken place in " the year when Emperor Maximilian established perpetual peace in Germany "—probably about the last year or so of the fifteenth century. The men appeared in tights and jerkins and the ladies in pánniered skirts and high powdered wigs. The whole effect must have been extremely funny, as the language of the production was certainly not that of the late Middle Ages.

Schiller's *Fiesco* and *Kabale und Liebe* were nothing like as popular as *The Robbers*. He also wrote *Don Carlos* and *Die Verschwörung* during the 'eighties, when he was appointed author to the National Theatre at Mannheim.

Goethe had already contributed *Clavigo* and *Stella* to the rapidly mounting collection of German dramatic works, before the 'eighties, and a general and warm interest in the theatre had replaced the half-hearted toleration with which it had previously been received.

Iffland was another great writer of this period, and his ideas ran to the painting of human life without character. His *Crime and Ambition* and *The Marksman* were his two best and most outstanding dramatic works.

The most prolific German dramatic writer of the century was A. von Kotzebue, who seems to have positively steeped Germany in the multitudinous efforts that he poured forth between 1790 and 1800. *Armuth und Edelsinn* was produced nearly every year from 1795 to 1822. Though to the modern mind his plays seem tedious and long-winded, they were undoubtedly popular in their own time and were frequently translated into other languages and produced in other countries within a few months of their original production in Germany.

It is due to Iffland to say that with him died the dramatic art of eighteenth-century Germany.

EIGHTEENTH-CENTURY DRESS

A HIGH, frilled head-dress called a 'pinner' had come into fashion in the late 'eighties of the preceding century.

The 'pinner' was a starched and sometimes, in more exaggerated interpretations, wired lace frill, fan-shaped and pleated. It was arranged on the front of the head in an upstanding crest. The frill might be single or double. In the latter case a row of looped ribbons stood up at equal intervals between the two frills; a cluster of ribbons, usually formally arranged, were placed at the back of the pinner. The whole arrangement of frills or ribbons was often sewn on to a little flat bonnet worn on the back of the head, and in this case it was called a 'commode.' Various additions, such as a hanging veil behind, or a narrow fringed scarf folded and stitched to the bonnet so that the fringed ends hung either at the back or over the shoulders, were very popular.

The height of the pinner-frill varied from a few inches to as much as eighteen inches in more exaggerated styles, and the difficulty of balancing this erection with dignity

(1700)

Fig. 41

was often lessened by the addition of a triangular, jewelled clasp fixed to the hair immediately above the forehead, and could be attached to the base of the frill, giving it a reasonably safe mooring.

The excessive height of these head-dresses was an object of great amusement to the satirists of the time, and when a shawl was worn over the head, an

FRENCH (1704)
Fig. 42

absurd silhouette was the result, as can be well imagined.
A contemporary writer of the time aptly describes the
effect in the couplet:

Whilst head was 'erst on shoulders placed
Imagine now about the waist.

VENETIAN (1710)
Fig. 43

FRENCH (1717)

Fig. 44

This was undoubtedly a fashion of French inspiration and was much worn in France and England during the 'nineties. Venetian and Spanish ladies had adopted them at the beginning of the eighteenth century and were several years later in discarding them than the Parisienne, who had completely lost interest in the 'commode' by 1710.

Almost with the opening year of the century French hair-fashion began to change; the pinner and its accompanying conglomeration of frills and ribbons, wire and lace was a thing of the past by 1710, and for a few hesitant years long curls vied in popularity with the novel idea of packing the hair away close to the head, and placing an absurd little lace cap on the top. The tendency towards an 'undressed' effect became a feature of the fashionable after 1715—and whether the effect was obtained by a pseudo-classical or pseudo-pastoral gown, informality was the attempted result.

This *négligé* was not confined entirely to women's clothes, for although the full-bottomed wigs and wired skirts to the coats were worn at Court by the fashionable

FRENCH (1720)
Fig. 45

gentleman, in his house he often preferred to wear his own hair or an embroidered cap over his shaven head. In French prints we may frequently find the neck of the shirt open, and the cravat either threaded through a button-hole or else completely discarded. Waistcoats were rarely fastened with more than two or three buttons out of the dozens that adorned them, and on the whole the effect was of a careless or untidy finish.

Women's formal wear included hoops at the side of the skirt to support the panniers, and by about 1718 the English fashion for a gigantic hooped skirt had arrived in Paris—a fashion to last for at least sixty years. The bodices remained tightly laced down the front but extremely low-cut. A loose all-enveloping gown was worn over the dress for informal occasions, and its popularity soon established it as a fashionable addition to the wardrobe. These gowns were called ' contouches ' and were gathered across the shoulders at the back, their fullness extending to envelope the huge hooped skirts beneath. The front was often left open, or tied with one or two bows of ribbon—an altogether charming style which Watteau has recorded for us in several of his delightful pictures of the early eighteenth century.

The sleeves of the formal gown had become tight-fitting from shoulder to elbow to finish in a deep, crumpled cuff which displayed several layers of fine lace worn on the garment beneath. But the more informal garments such as the ' contouche ' and short coat often had long-fitting sleeves or full-gathered ones from shoulder to wrist.

Square neck-lines, elbow-sleeves with deep lace frills, hooped skirts, and a tightly laced waist finishing in a V-front remained standard features of the gowns from about 1715 to 1770, although details altered considerably from

FRENCH (1718)
Fig. 46

time to time. The most striking and noticeable alteration in fashion was in the hairdressing.

Between 1710 and 1740 these changes were slight but nevertheless noticeable, and it is often from these alterations that, in pictures and prints, a gown otherwise undated can be definitely placed.

By 1715 the hair was generally packed away, inconspicuously, and probably often cut short so that it should make a suitably small head to top the gigantic, hooped skirts. A curious feature of these hooped skirts is that each time the fashion for farthingales, hoops, or crinolines arrived, the style of head-dress assumed a compact and bijou effect in almost ridiculous contrast to the excessive width beneath. During the 'thirties the ends of the hair were often arranged to form small curls which covered the back of the head; the size of the cap was definitely larger, and by the 'forties it had obtained the proportions of a mob-cap. Curls were now generally visible, and, during the 'forties, ringlets were frequently worn, peeping out in clusters beneath the large pseudo-peasant hat, which in its turn was worn over a cap. A temporary and charming informality in hairdressing was fostered by the craze in the French Court for imitating the simplicity of styles worn by shepherds and shepherdesses. It was during the 'fifties that women began to follow the masculine fashion for powdering the hair, and a more definite and formal style of hairdressing inspired the first genius among

(1740)   (1770)

Fig. 47

FRENCH (1730)
Fig. 48

FRENCH (1735)
Fig. 49

barbers to introduce once again a fashion that women could not follow without the assistance of a qualified hairdresser. Little by little the fashion developed into the peculiar absurdities of the late 'seventies and 'eighties. The variety of mere hair-arrangement, supplemented by horse hair, padding, wire frames, false switches, pomatum, and powder, failed to be sufficiently amusing when every one indulged in the same mad experiments. Then absurdly exaggerated wigs added height and width to the fashion, and the variety of arrangements of curls—even from the imperfect records that we still have of the fashions—are bewilderingly numerous. Curls piled in sausage-like rolls, flatly clustered at the back of the wig, and rolled in or out on the neck; long curls and short curls arranged over the shoulders; great hoops held up on top of the piled head or looped low at the back of the neck—all are represented.

Strings of pearls, feathers, and flowers, and little laced and beribboned caps decorated the less extreme hair arrangements. But eventually these styles failed to be sufficiently striking, and every one who had any pretensions to be thought fashionable indulged in the crazy experiments of adding ornament to an already over-decorated head. Ornaments became even more important than the hair or wig, and ladies vied with one another to outdo the possibilities of exaggeration in this direction.

France was not alone in this fashion; for every country entered into the weird and exciting competition. While gigantic ostrich plumes and strings of pearls might be worn by a German princess, a lady with a sense of humour and a fertile imagination appeared in Paris with a roundabout on her head complete with striped awning and flags, and a Spanish galleon in full sail sailed blissfully on a sea of

GERMAN (1767) FRENCH (1772)

Fig. 50

white curls, perched on the head of an enterprising señorita.

Europe undoubtedly felt the effects of these fresh absurdities, and architects had to take into consideration the fact that a normally tall woman encumbered by a head-dress three feet or more in height must be able to sweep with dignity through doorways and not be compelled to bend a towering head at an inconvenient moment. Not only must the door be high but wide also, as skirts hooped out sideways might quite easily be eight feet wide. By the end of the 'seventies, however, the towering, top-heavy wigs and decoration proved so inconvenient and insanitary that a new style had to be devised. Germany and some of the less enterprising countries still continued to wear the monstrosities of the 'seventies for a further ten years or more, but French ladies, for the few remaining years before the Revolution, wore their hair in a thick and frizzed mass of curls, cut to various lengths and puffed and padded so as to form a vast curly surround to the face and shoulders. The hair was still dressed high, but its height was now balanced by its width and the tumbling rolls of curls that covered the shoulders. Hats of gigantic proportions and decorated to an absurd degree again became necessary furnishings for the fashionable lady.

As I have previously mentioned, the line of the skirt frequently follows the shape of the hairdressing. The one is certainly influenced by the other, and during the 'eighties and 'nineties of the eighteenth century, this fact is perhaps even more obvious than at any other period. In the early years of the 'eighties skirts remained full but not obviously hooped. The panniered skirts were held out with the assistance of crumpled paper and corded petticoats. There was a definite tendency towards a bustle. The hair also was assisted in its fullness by padding and horse hair, but no longer arranged over a wire frame. Curls did not fall much below the shoulders, and the back of the head was more padded than the top. By about 1784 a train had appeared at the back of the 'bustled' skirt, and the hair at the back was drawn down and curled in a separate roll, which often reached quite a distance down the back. Two years later the skirt ceased to be bunched and padded, except at the back. Fashion demanded an S-shaped figure—and a straight line from the breast downward. Trains were quite the usual thing for a well-dressed Frenchwoman, and the whole silhouette was more formal and less decorated. As far as possible the latest hair-styles followed this line. The hair was puffed and curled over the forehead and formally arranged in curls at the

FRENCH (1790)
Fig. 51

back and sides, with long sweeping S-shaped locks hanging down the back almost to the waist.

Quite suddenly in 1796 the formalities of the previous decade vanished. The bustle and corsets were cast aside, the wigs and fantastically arranged hairdressing disappeared, to be followed by the startlingly undressed and shorn effect of short hair and transparent, high-waisted gowns. The differences between the gowns of 1795 and 1796 are almost as surprising as the differences in hairdressing. It is almost incredible that such a startling contrast should occur in apparently only a few months.

The shadow of the Revolution had been successfully evaded by the casting aside of all that remained as a reminder. Not one detail of women's dress remained the same—even shoes and gloves had altered—the little heels that had been so popular throughout the century were succeeded by flat-soled pumps tied round the ankles with ribbons. The short wrist-length gloves had been entirely superseded by long ones that reached almost to the shoulder, covering the otherwise exposed arm. Huge hats had been replaced by diminutive and child-like bonnets.

Where the tight-corseted waist-line had been there was now merely a gay ribbon tied beneath the breasts. The full skirts with a bunch behind were an absurdity of the past, and ladies vied with one another in wearing the most daringly revealing skirts of diaphanous materials that blew caressingly around their uncovered legs. By 1799 the gown had become so skimpy that they were often cut up the side to allow a little more freedom for walking, and chamois-leather tights had to be worn as some sort of unobtrusive covering against the inclemencies of the weather—a covering, indeed, that did not interfere with the clinging line of the skirts which was so necessary to a well-dressed Frenchwoman. These extremes, however, did not penetrate to other countries. The general adoption of ' Empire ' styles was considerably modified, although the main factors and lines remained the same or similar. The attempted effect of semi-nudity—termed ' classic '— was essentially of Parisian inspiration, and although a pseudo-classic influence was copied by practically every other European country, the extreme *décolleté* line was often covered by a *modestie,* and the clinging skirts rendered less revealing by a petticoat beneath.

FRENCH (1734)
Fig. 52

The shape of the corset of the eighteenth century did not vary to anything like the degree of that of the seventeenth. Within ten years or so of the beginning of the century the very stiff, high stays had been supplanted by a kind which, though still laced tightly to the waist, did not materially interfere with nature's original plans for the feminine form. The gowns were all boned from breast to waist and usually finished by lacing down the front to a slight V. This shape remained unchanged until the 'sixties, when the waist-line gradually dropped to a few inches below the normal and the V-front was slightly more exaggerated. Throughout the 'seventies tight lacing became more and more usual until, once again, in the 'eighties, we find the tiny waist and the breasts forced upward, thus fostering a fashion for a pigeon-breasted effect which was exaggerated by the addition of stiffened fichus and frilled and flowered collars.

One remarkable feature of women's attire, that re-mained with very few exceptions universally fashionable, was the eighteenth-century sleeve, tight fitting from shoulder to elbow and terminating in an excessive display of layered lace frills or fine, embroidered lawn, gathered and arranged so that the layers fell away from the elbow almost to the wrist. Bows of ribbon and goffered frills were usually worn just above the lace frills, and some-times, following the masculine fashions of the time, cuffs were worn.

Sleeves became popular soon after the beginning of the century and remained in favour for about ninety years, when they were eventually supplanted by the tight-fitting long sleeve or the extremely short one so typical of Empire fashion.

During the 'twenties and 'thirties, when the contouche and loose-fitting over-gowns were so very popular, the

FRENCH (1740)
Fig. 53

sleeve was not always close fitting, but gathered slightly at the shoulder to give plenty of space for the sleeve beneath. These sleeves either terminated in a deep, soft cuff—an informal edition of the masculine fashion—or else were finished with a slightly wider opening, longer over the elbow point than in front. There are a few examples of the sleeve being very full and gathered both at shoulder and below the elbow, forming a loose bag to accommodate the frills beneath. This was probably so that the wearer could comfortably tuck away her layers of lace frills so that they

ITALIAN (1750)
Fig. 54

should not get unduly in the way while she busied herself about domestic duties.

In eighteenth-century paintings there are to be found perhaps about half a dozen styles which are exceptions to the elbow sleeve with frills. One of these is the rather charming frilled sleeve which was worn sometimes during the 'forties and 'fifties. This consisted of numerous layers of tiny frills from shoulder to just below the elbow. A long, tight sleeve was rarely worn, though practically all the coats were made with a close-fitting long sleeve.

Probably, owing to the extreme fullness of the frilled ' cuff,' coats were rarely worn. Cloaks, short capes, and a sacque-backed over-gown were more often to be seen before the 'twenties.

During the 'seventies and early 'eighties a fuller though still short sleeve was almost as popular as the older style. It was decorated with one or two tiny frills and finished at the elbow, with no hanging lace ' cuff.'

Italian ladies were slow to follow the Parisian fashion, and we may find that almost throughout the century their fashions are modified and that they are several years behind in adopting or discarding the new or old styles, as the case might be.

One obvious and fascinating fashion that was essentially Venetian in its inspiration, and only Italian in interpretation, was the adoption of vast Venetian cloaks. Hoods surrounded the face and covered the shoulders, and the tricorne hat was worn over the hood. These three items were as popular for men as for ladies.

The cloaks continued to be worn until the nineteenth century, but the hats and hoods were of necessity abandoned when the wigs became too high and ornate to

VENETIAN (1745)
Fig. 55

accommodate them comfortably. After that date—some time in the 'seventies—vast, concealing black shawls were worn, as extreme secrecy was necessary to a Venetian lady who followed the conventional intrigue which was so much part of the everyday life of the eighteenth century. Masks were fashionable in Spain and Italy as a further disguise when necessary, and fans were an important part of my lady's wardrobe, both as an enhancement for her sparkling eyes and as a shelter from a too penetrating gaze. The use of a fan to a lady was as much of an art as the use of snuff for a gentleman, and from the 'eighties of the seventeenth century until almost the close of the eighteenth these toys were so much a part of fashionable life that they might almost be considered an item of apparel. Many fans and snuff-boxes were works of art, the most famous artists of the times being employed to paint upon these elegant pieces of frippery. Fans were made of both silk and chicken-skin and often had designs on both sides. Snuff-boxes—which had to appear frequently in use—were more often made of enamels and silver and gold filigree-work, though there are many examples of hand-painted ones still to be found.

If we consider for a moment the decoration of skirts —which dated them far more surely than their actual shape—we can see that at the beginning of the century the split front with contrasting panel was more usual than one that was made of the same material all round. Tiny aprons were very much the vogue from about 1730, and from being merely an addition to the skirt, they eventually became the most decorative part of it. During the 'forties and 'fifties, when materials were either embroidered or printed all over, the obvious method of using a plain material for the apron in contrast was not adopted, because

FRENCH (1762)
Fig. 56

MARIE ANTOINETTE (1770)
Fig. 57

it immediately gave the impression of serving a useful and practical purpose which was not its function. We find, therefore, many examples of checked or striped material or very fine and exquisite silk embroideries on these diaphanous pieces of nonsense. Their purpose was so essentially ornamental that they were more often than not actually sewn on to the skirt at the time that it was made.

As the size of the skirts was so extreme, hand-embroideries on the gowns themselves were unusual, and ladies found that the apron was just a convenient size and shape to embroider with delicacy. Similarly, the embroideries on coats were always on the cuffs and pocket-flaps—small pieces that could be carried around with ease and

GERMAN (1775)
Fig. 58

comfort. The supports of the immense skirts changed in the 'sixties from being a hoop or hoops of whalebone into steel or bamboo ovals worn over each hip. Several curious devices for skirt-supports appeared at this time. There were those that hinged up and down from the hips to facilitate going through small doorways or getting into sedan chairs.

As the shape changed, the decorations altered from all-over patterns to the more fashionable method of adorning the skirt with dozens of yards of gathered and pleated ribbons, tassels, and even feathers. Quite often an over-skirt of some fragile and transparent material, such as dotted muslin, was worn over a silk or satin skirt, and gathered up with running cords or ribbons to fall in a series of curved folds to the bottom of the gown. These transparent over-skirts first came into vogue several years earlier. As an interesting innovation for ballet-costumes, they were quite frequently worn on ball-gowns as early as the 'fifties, though more popular still during the 'sixties and 'seventies. During the 'seventies floral decoration was not nearly so popular as it had been, and ladies let their fancy have its way with the assistance of ribbon and lace and frills.

It was in the early years of the 'eighties that the most amazing effects were obtained from the use of pleated frills and gathered ribbon, combined with the new idea for looping up an overskirt over a mass of crushed paper or bunched taffeta. As these skirts were often short enough to display the ankle, the effect was a curiously unbalanced one. With huge heads and gigantic bonnets or hats went tiny waists and padded breasts pushed up almost to the chin, and large over-decorated skirts finishing in two tiny ankles and feet. This was fortunately a fashion of short duration, for the re-introduction of trains immediately

GERMAN (1780)
Fig. 59

FRENCH (1780)
Fig. 60

detracted from the interest in skirt-decoration, while ladies racked their well-covered brains for new and enchanting colour-schemes for the bustled and trained gowns of the early 'nineties.

The comparative sobriety that enveloped France for a few years during and after the Revolution was noticeable only in the discarding of unnecessary and too blatant ornamentation. The new figure-shape was still very silly and unpractical, as is shown in fashion-plates of the time. These must always be treated with reserve, however, as indeed must our modern fashion-plates, which would possibly give our great-grandchildren the impression that we were a race of hipless giants with legs of incredible length.

The concept we form when the eighteenth century is mentioned is of elegant, satin-clad gentlemen with white wigs, tricorne hats, knee-breeches, full-skirted coats, and buckled shoes. In reality, there were even more changes in masculine fashions during the eighteenth century than there were in feminine ones. The tricorne hat and the buckled shoes were the only details that were worn throughout the century, and both of these changed their shape considerably during that period.

The century opened with the huge full-bottomed wigs, so popular during the closing years of the preceding century. This popularity lasted for some ten years, when the exaggeratedly stiff styles were eventually abandoned for the far more comfortable craze for informality and a pseudo-peasant or pastoral style. This revulsion was probably considerably encouraged by the fashion for ' classic ' simplicity which, though undoubtedly bogus and absurdly interpreted, was in theory a spirited attempt to break away from the forced stiffness and excessive decoration

FRENCH (1710)
Fig. 61

of the seventeenth-century French Court. Every one who could read acquired a superficial knowledge of the Greek classic and mythological literature, and the simplicity of the ancient pastoral life with its naïve and charming frankness made an undoubted appeal to the minds of those who had been reared in an atmosphere of intrigue and camouflage.

The coarse realism of a peasant's life was not, however, allowed to interfere with the elegant and fragrant translation that suited the contemporary attitude. The nearest model that presented itself to the fastidious French noble was found in the decorative and colourful groupings of the strolling players. Their simple charm had been much enhanced by the paintings of Watteau and Legrand, and when once more troupes were allowed to appear in Paris, many of their costumes—which were frankly left-overs from the preceding century—were copied and worn by the classic-minded gallant and his lady.

Wigs of course were the first 'unnatural' features to be discarded, but as so many men had shorn heads for the convenience of accommodating wigs, a compromise had to be made by the wearing of a neat white wig curled in front and finishing with a queue or 'bag' behind. Others, who had not gone to the extreme of shaving their heads, wore their hair loose to the shoulder or tied back with

FRENCH (1749)
Fig. 62

a ribbon. Often the hair was powdered as a convenient camouflage if false hair had to be attached.

High heels were the next extravagance to be abandoned, and the use of jewels and metal and gold and silver embroideries was replaced by elegant floral designs embroidered on both coats and waistcoats. The rather bright and heavy colours which had been so popular a few years earlier were entirely discarded in favour of pastel tints.

Pinks, blues, yellows, mauves, cyclamen, and white were, fashionable if not practical shades. Whether it was the exquisite embroideries and designs worked on the waist-coats that encouraged gentlemen to discard their coats for informal occasions, or whether the stiffened cuffs and wired skirts of their coats were unsuited to the elegant occupation of dancing and lolling in their lovely gardens, it is impossible at this date to ascertain. Whatever the reason, there are numerous examples of the negligent fashion which displayed the beauty of the waistcoat and the frilled and elegantly gathered shirt-sleeve and cravat to the appreciative eyes of their lady friends.

The shape of the coat remained almost the same for some fifty years—wide-cuffed and full-skirted with much-embroidered pockets and no collar. It was during the 'fifties that the fullness of the skirts began to collapse, and the fashion for smaller cuffs showed the first tendency towards the complete abandonment of these features twenty years later.

About 1730 the Frenchman began to wear his knee-breeches over his stockings, rolled down to just above the knee, where previously the fashion had been to garter them just below the knee.

This new fashion led to the introduction of fancy buckles worn on the outside of the knee where previously a bow of ribbon had adorned the garter.

The simplicity of the first white wigs and powdered natural hair soon wore off, and a variety of formal arrangements that included layers of sausage-like curls at either side of the face soon became the order of the day. Many gentlemen wore their own hair long in front and powdered, brushed backward, and rolled over a wig which was cleverly hidden in the curled front-pieces. This added to

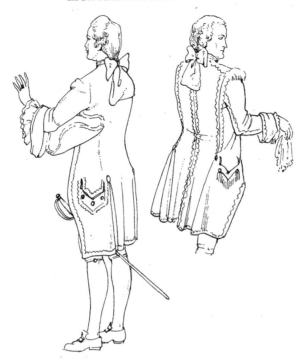

FRENCH (1779)
Fig. 63

the fashionable ' sleekness ' of the back of the head, while the hair framing the face was required to curl.

Soon after 1760 the coat underwent a radical change. The front was cut back to form a curve, and while it displayed large quantities of waistcoat in front, the coat fell into flat folds at the back. Though the coat ' skirts ' still remained in three separate pieces for a further eight or ten years, they were a mere apology for the skirts of a previous decade. Gradually they were cut shorter and shorter. The waistcoat, too, became shorter, until in 1770 it finished at the hips, the last few buttons being left undone to form

VENETIAN (1782)
Fig. 64

an inverted V-shape. In 1770 coats of the extreme fashion
only just covered the buttocks at the back and were not
visible from the front below the pockets, which had risen
considerably from their original position to just below the
waist.

The Frenchman's fashions of the 'seventies were even

more fantastic than those of the ladies. It was at this particular period that the Macaronis made their appearance with their striped stockings, long tight knee-breeches, short coats, striped waistcoats, absurdly high cravats, and high piled wigs surmounted by a ridiculous little tricorne hat only a few inches in size.

The most striking feature of the extreme fashions of the 'seventies was the great tightness of fit and a brevity which undoubtedly gave a definite impression of a child outgrowing his clothes.

Where previously the coats had hung full and in flattering lines, they were now frequently cut away so much in the front that it was quite impossible to fasten the buttons. The sleeves were extremely tight and finished a few inches above the wrist so that the frilled shirt might still be visible. The back of the coat gave the impression of a beetle with its wings folded tightly back. Collars on coats had arrived during the 'sixties. They were, however, quite small and were sometimes worn turned up, completely covering the cravat at the back of the neck.

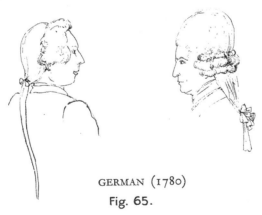

GERMAN (1780)

Fig. 65.

The knee-breeches, which were now so very much more exposed by the cut-away coats and short waistcoats, were worn extremely tight-fitting, and often reached several inches below the knee, being fastened with buttons.

For a few years barbers struggled to make the masculine wig and hairdressing as complicated as that of women, and several amusing exaggerations appeared in conse-

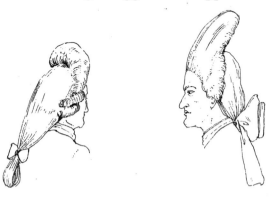

GERMAN (1780)
Fig. 66

quence. Wire frames and horse-hair went to the filling out of the high wig. Layers of complicated curls were arranged at the sides and a series of loops or an exaggeratedly long queue appeared at the back. More frequently only the front part of the hair was raised, while at the back a sleekness was encouraged—which terminated in a huge bow of ribbon.

These extreme styles lasted for five or six years only, and before the 'eighties the masculine wig had assumed quite reasonable proportions. The tight, short coats had been discarded in preference to one nearly reaching to the knees. It could still be curved in front with a beetle back or remain a collapsed and elongated version of the coats of

GERMAN (1785)
Fig. 67

FRENCH (1784)
Fig. 68

the 'sixties. The collar, however, had come to stay; and experimental cutting soon led to the introduction of *revers*. The fashion for buttoning the front of the curved coats soon suggested to the tailor a new shape. This was for the cut-away coat with tails, which made its first appear-

GERMAN (1785)
Fig. 69

GERMAN (1786)
Fig. 70

ance during the 'eighties. We can still recognize its direct descendant in the formal evening dress of to-day.

It was during the 'eighties that yet another wave of simplicity occurred. This was fostered by Marie Antoinette's interest in the ' Arcadians '; once more this was very much of a pseudo-pastoral affair, and its effect upon the extravagances of the French Court was almost negligible. It did perhaps account for the discarding of the hoops in the ladies' skirts and the newer fashion of pannier and bustle effects which were considered to be in the shepherdess manner. Quite probably it exterminated—or helped to exterminate—the absurdly exaggerated men's fashions of the 'seventies. This pastoralism was entirely of French origin and did not materially affect other countries. Germany, in particular, after having adopted the absurdities and exaggerations of the 'seventies, found it extremely difficult to discard them, and there are many examples of the masculine high wig and the over-decorated hooped skirts being worn in Germany five or even ten years after they had been discarded in France.

Except for evening and dress occasions the richly embroidered coat had been replaced by a fashion for plain materials during the 'sixties, and so that the coat should not appear unduly severe, colours were very much brighter and stronger than they had been for some seventy years. Binding and coloured borders were quite frequently used on coats, but the chief garment to receive attention was the waistcoat, which was either striped in gay contrasting colours or embroidered all over. Colour contrasts played an important part in men's dress until the Revolution, which effectively put a stop to anything too striking or too gay and noticeable. Blacks, greys, browns, dark blues, and other drab shades were suitably inconspicuous. Wigs were discarded, and a fashion for wearing the hair cut short to the ears in a sort of untidy bob became a simple and practical solution of masculine hairdressing. By 1790 the silks and satins, fine wigs, and rich embroideries were things of the past. The tricorne hat had been replaced by a stiff high-crowned hat with a brim curved up at each side and adorned by a large buckle in front. The cloth coat with its cut-away front and long tails displayed a handsome waistcoat and a watch-fob hanging from the watch-pocket of the trousers. Tall boots encased the stockinged legs. The whole effect—measured by modern standards—was one more masculine than had previously been secured. Certainly the clothes offered a better resistance to wind and rain, though to a generation that had been reared to silks, satins, and velvets, the cloth and linen must have seemed dreadfully plain, coarse, and homely.

As in previous centuries fashions in design and embroidery played an important part in dating certain garments. The century opened with heavy, stiff brocade, richly enhanced with jewels and gold and silver embroideries; from about 1715 the preference for fine floral embroideries on equally fine and brilliant satins and velvets became the order of the day, and for some thirty years or more coats and waistcoats were adorned with leaf-designs or flowers twined in and out upon a curled branch, which became more luxurious over pockets, on the corners of coats, and, of course, on cuffs.

The increased interest in importations from the East provoked a desire for Oriental patterns and colours during the 'forties and 'fifties, and larger designs frequently spread all over coat or waistcoat, the pattern being picked out once more in both gold and silver thread. Cut velvets, embossed satins, all-over embroidery which

FRENCH (1798)
Fig. 71

tried to copy the richly decorated coats worn by Chinese mandarins and other Eastern dignitaries were fashionable throughout Europe. The reason for the abandonment of these richly ornamented garments in preference to the tight-fitting and graceless little coats of the 'seventies is not exactly clear. Possibly it was merely due to a swing of the pendulum of fashion. Change was desired, and therefore it was found necessary to devise a shape entirely different. It certainly could not have been the outcome of a revulsion against extravagance, because the fashions of the early 'seventies were perhaps the silliest and most absurdly unpractical of all periods. Satirists devised endless pleasure and amusement from observing the stilted mincing manners of the effeminate and elegant fop dressed in towering wig and glove-like fit of coat and breeches. At this period design was limited to the edges of the coat or waistcoat, for those who still wished to flaunt embroideries, but by far the most typical pattern of the time was stripes—horizontal or vertical stripes, usually on a white ground, decorated stockings and waistcoats, sometimes even coats, though in the latter case the stripes were usually much closer together. After the 'seventies embroideries were once more fashionable for a few years, until the Revolution, which of course made such display positively dangerous. After that date design and pattern practically disappeared as a masculine feature of everyday dress, and women were left with a complete monopoly of figured materials, silks, satins, and embroideries. Dull and dark colours remained popular for men's clothes from that date to this, although the closing years of the eighteenth century and the early years of the nineteenth did at least show the charm of contrast in the coloured coat and white breeches, or a black coat and coloured breeches. It was not until seventy years later that complete uniformity of both colour and cut robbed the male of any possible display of individuality in his choice of clothing.

It was, however, during the 'nineties that the standard features of modern masculine dress were definitely established, and cloth coats became a necessary feature of everyday wear. Silks and satins were discarded as an effeminate and unmanly habit, only fit for evening dress and Court functions. This theory, which still obviously exists, can quite definitely be dated from the French Revolution, and though other countries clung for a few more years to the more cheerful and colourful materials of an earlier decade, France had definitely turned her back on all those things that had helped the aristocrat to display his wealth in his manner of dress.

THE BEGINNING OF THE NINETEENTH CENTURY

THE nineteenth century started with the fundament: changes in costume already made. Slim Empir gowns, shorn heads, large bonnets, and flat shoes for th ladies, and tall hats, skin-fitting breeches, tailed coats, an short waistcoats for the men.

One of the first changes of the nineteenth century wa from knee-breeches to trousers. Knee-breeches had bee gradually getting longer and longer, and the earlie: trousers were simply very long knee-breeches—buttonin from the knee to the calf. Fashion decreed that they shoul be skin-tight, and quite often this form of exaggeratio was carried to such an extreme that the ' dandy ' of th period wore chamois-leather trousers which did not allo sufficient room to sit down comfortably. Breeches fc ' strolling ' were changed for a more ' roomy ' pair whe the ' dandy ' had to take tea sitting down.

Long boots and gaiters reaching above the knee prc tected the stockings from the inclemencies of the weathe and served for walking and riding in the still very mudd and dusty roads, but by 1810 the knee-breeches had con pletely disappeared, except for evening and Court wea: They were, however, still worn by those sufficiently olc fashioned to cherish a style that had become almost tradition for over a century.

As the breeches grew longer, the collars and cravat became higher, and soon after 1810 a high stiff collar wa adopted instead of the yards of material previously en ployed for a cravat. The cravat itself, though still worr

(1808)
Fig. 72

was no longer the chief form of neckwear, but had assumed the inferior position of a tie. Wound round the neck in several lengths, it tied in front in a bow over the tall wings of the stiff collar which in extreme styles came right up over the ears and reached to the cheek-bones.

The fashion for *revers* which had started several years earlier had become an absolute obsession a few years after the new century began. These were cut in all manner of shapes, but they always finished with a very high collar at the back of the coat. This emphasis on the neck gave the men of the time a curious effect of sloping shoulders, which is not really to be wondered at, considering the variety of collars, cravats, and waistcoat collars that were packed tightly up to the ears. Frilled shirts with ruffles for throat and waist were fashionable until about 1820— as long, in fact, as the cut-away coat remained open in front to reveal the waistcoat and shirt. About 1820 a new full-skirted coat which buttoned at the waist was introduced, and when this was not worn the cut-away coat was double-breasted. Trousers having become an accepted fashion—several variations from the straight cut were introduced—the most amusing and obvious of these were the peg-top trousers. These were frilled or gathered at the hips, with a tight-fitting waist, and fairly tight from knee to ankle, where they were kept down with the aid of a strap under the shoe. French styles carried the fashion to absurdity with padded and even wired-out hips. The fashion lasted with modifications from about 1820 to 1835. It was probably due to their ungainly shape that the coats had to change. The double-breasted coats of the late 'twenties had full, well-curved tails, while the skirted coats were tight-waisted and flared from the hips to below the knees. The peg-top trousers never became evening wear.

The skin-fitting trousers, reaching to within a few inches of the ankle and accentuating the curve of the calf, were always worn for dancing until well into the 'thirties.

The man's hat, which for so long had been a standard tricorne, when once changed, went through a variety of shapes and sizes until eventually it settled down into the accepted 'top hat' of the nineteenth century.

Probably the most obvious of these transitional styles were the cocked hat of the early years of the century and the huge curled-brimmed 'topper' of the 'twenties or the tall 'chimney-pot' type which found favour from about 1820 to 1840. One of the old fashions that still clung included the 'caped' coat, or highwayman's cloak, which served so useful a purpose in protecting the wearer's shoulders from rain that it was worn by coachmen for several decades after it had disappeared from the average wardrobe.

By 1840 all the familiar appurtenances of the twentieth-century gentleman had made their appearance—the trousers, short waistcoat, cloth coat, shirt, stiff collar, tie, and top hat !

Although it appears at first glance that women's clothes made such striking changes during the first forty years of the nineteenth century, the changes

FRENCH (1807)
Fig. 73

FRENCH (1807)
Fig. 74

FRENCH (1817)
Fig. 75

were gradual. Skirts slowly shortened and became wider at the hems. The high waist-line dropped gently, an inch at a time, until, about twenty-five years after the beginning of the century, it had once more reached the normal position.

FRENCH (1823)
Fig. 76

FRENCH (1824)
Fig. 77

Hairdressing probably showed the most striking changes, because for some fifteen years the hair had been worn short, and then after various experiments it appeared in the fantastic styles of the early 'thirties, piled high and knotted into absurd shapes, decorated with flowers and ribbons, lace, and pearls. For just one decade it was held up by wire frames and embellished with false switches. Then the fashion collapsed as suddenly as it had appeared, and was replaced by the sober middle parting and bobbing curls of the late 'thirties.

The clinging pseudo-Greek lines of the early Empire gown had changed into rather an unsophisticated little-girl dress by about 1805. High-waisted and with skirts above the ankles, gathered at the waist, puffed sleeves, flat shoes, a large bonnet, and the merest apology for a coat all made a becoming fashion for the very young, but the older woman must have welcomed the fuller-skirted, high-necked, and longer-sleeved gowns of ten years later. Between 1815 and 1823 a perfectly delightful phase of fashion existed. Skirts were full at the bottom and worn just off the ground, waists were still high, but not too high. A military fashion favoured cords and frogs as trimmings; large, feathered

FRENCH (1824)
Fig. 78

(1828)
Fig. 79

bonnets and hats were also rather military in style. Hairdressing was simple and favoured natural charm. There
was no shadow of the absurdities of the late 'twenties
visible until about 1824, when tight-lacing became obvious.

One of fashion's inevitable demands is that when the
waist is constricted the shoulders must be padded and

FRENCH (1830)
Fig. 80

wired and the skirts must shoot out from the tiny waist as quickly and as briefly as possible ! By 1830 shoulders had become monstrosities in their excess of padding. Ruffles had appeared to cover the neck. Huge hats bearing every conceivable ribbon, flower, fruit, and feather were balanced precariously on the towering curled confection of hairdressing that had supplanted any attempts at natural charm. Skirts were short, displaying the boot and perhaps

FRENCH (1832)
Fig. 81

even an inch or so of stocking, and very, very full. No hoop had yet been inserted, but stiffened petticoats and crino-zephyr, which was a sort of horse-hair tissue, were usually worn.

Starch played a very important and uncomfortable part in the laundering of the 'thirties. Starched ruffles, cuffs, collars, and petticoats were indispensable, and the gigantic puffed sleeves were often assisted by wire supports or little feather pillows.

However, by about 1838 these absurd excesses had died down in the eventual adoption of the crinoline silhouette, which was to be popular for so many years. The tight-fitting bodice, huge hooped skirt, shawl, and poke-bonnet, so dear to the heart of the romanticist and to the designer of Christmas cards—all these had arrived to stay for a quarter of a century.

During the early years of the nineteenth century ladies wore the palest of colours, white and pastel shades being great favourites, but soon after 1810 purples, deep reds, golds, and violent blues became extremely fashionable for little coats, hats, and scarves, and by 1820 colour was brilliant and striking for practically every costume or occasion.

Even the dinner-gowns and ball-dresses were of dark or bright colours. Heaviness was seen, not only in cut and design, but in everything. Plaids and large pattens were particularly fashionable during the 'thirties, although there was also a temporary craze for them as early as 1810.

As has already been mentioned, colour was fast fading from the wardrobe of the male. Deep greens, dark blue, brown, and of course black were all popular for coats; trousers were nearly always of a lighter shade. Reds, violets, yellows, and pinks had completely vanished, except for an occasional waistcoat, as early as 1810.

A few colours were still to be seen in the ballrooms—in embroidered satin coats—but by about 1825 even dress-wear, the last stronghold of masculine elegance, was eventually overcome by the strength of neutrality—and the fine peacock that graced the ballrooms of the eighteenth century was replaced by the penguin of the nineteenth and twentieth.

INDEX

A CATALOG OF SELECTED DOVER
BOOKS IN ALL FIELDS OF INTEREST

CONCERNING THE SPIRITUAL IN ART, Wassily Kandinsky. Pioneering work by father of abstract art. Thoughts on color theory, nature of art. Analysis of earlier masters. 12 illustrations. 80pp. of text. 5⅜ x 8½.   23411-8

ANIMALS: 1,419 Copyright-Free Illustrations of Mammals, Birds, Fish, Insects, etc., Jim Harter (ed.). Clear wood engravings present, in extremely lifelike poses, over 1,000 species of animals. One of the most extensive pictorial sourcebooks of its kind. Captions. Index. 284pp. 9 x 12.   23766-4

CELTIC ART: The Methods of Construction, George Bain. Simple geometric techniques for making Celtic interlacements, spirals, Kells-type initials, animals, humans, etc. Over 500 illustrations. 160pp. 9 x 12. (Available in U.S. only.)   22923-8

AN ATLAS OF ANATOMY FOR ARTISTS, Fritz Schider. Most thorough reference work on art anatomy in the world. Hundreds of illustrations, including selections from works by Vesalius, Leonardo, Goya, Ingres, Michelangelo, others. 593 illustrations. 192pp. 7⅛ x 10¼.   20241-0

CELTIC HAND STROKE-BY-STROKE (Irish Half-Uncial from "The Book of Kells"): An Arthur Baker Calligraphy Manual, Arthur Baker. Complete guide to creating each letter of the alphabet in distinctive Celtic manner. Covers hand position, strokes, pens, inks, paper, more. Illustrated. 48pp. 8¼ x 11.   24336-2

EASY ORIGAMI, John Montroll. Charming collection of 32 projects (hat, cup, pelican, piano, swan, many more) specially designed for the novice origami hobbyist. Clearly illustrated easy-to-follow instructions insure that even beginning papercrafters will achieve successful results. 48pp. 8¼ x 11.   27298-2

THE COMPLETE BOOK OF BIRDHOUSE CONSTRUCTION FOR WOOD-WORKERS, Scott D. Campbell. Detailed instructions, illustrations, tables. Also data on bird habitat and instinct patterns. Bibliography. 3 tables. 63 illustrations in 15 figures. 48pp. 5¼ x 8½.   24407-5

BLOOMINGDALE'S ILLUSTRATED 1886 CATALOG: Fashions, Dry Goods and Housewares, Bloomingdale Brothers. Famed merchants' extremely rare catalog depicting about 1,700 products: clothing, housewares, firearms, dry goods, jewelry, more. Invaluable for dating, identifying vintage items. Also, copyright-free graphics for artists, designers. Co-published with Henry Ford Museum & Greenfield Village. 160pp. 8¼ x 11.   25780-0

HISTORIC COSTUME IN PICTURES, Braun & Schneider. Over 1,450 costumed figures in clearly detailed engravings—from dawn of civilization to end of 19th century. Captions. Many folk costumes. 256pp. 8⅜ x 11¾.   23150-X

FRANK LLOYD WRIGHT'S DANA HOUSE, Donald Hoffmann. Pictorial essay of residential masterpiece with over 160 interior and exterior photos, plans, elevations, sketches and studies. 128pp. 9¼ x 10¾. 29120-0

THE MALE AND FEMALE FIGURE IN MOTION: 60 Classic Photographic Sequences, Eadweard Muybridge. 60 true-action photographs of men and women walking, running, climbing, bending, turning, etc., reproduced from rare 19th-century masterpiece. vi + 121pp. 9 x 12. 24745-7

1001 QUESTIONS ANSWERED ABOUT THE SEASHORE, N. J. Berrill and Jacquelyn Berrill. Queries answered about dolphins, sea snails, sponges, starfish, fishes, shore birds, many others. Covers appearance, breeding, growth, feeding, much more. 305pp. 5¼ x 8¼. 23366-9

ATTRACTING BIRDS TO YOUR YARD, William J. Weber. Easy-to-follow guide offers advice on how to attract the greatest diversity of birds: birdhouses, feeders, water and waterers, much more. 96pp. 5³⁄₁₆ x 8¼. 28927-3

MEDICINAL AND OTHER USES OF NORTH AMERICAN PLANTS: A Historical Survey with Special Reference to the Eastern Indian Tribes, Charlotte Erichsen-Brown. Chronological historical citations document 500 years of usage of plants, trees, shrubs native to eastern Canada, northeastern U.S. Also complete identifying information. 343 illustrations. 544pp. 6½ x 9¼. 25951-X

STORYBOOK MAZES, Dave Phillips. 23 stories and mazes on two-page spreads: Wizard of Oz, Treasure Island, Robin Hood, etc. Solutions. 64pp. 8¼ x 11. 23628-5

AMERICAN NEGRO SONGS: 230 Folk Songs and Spirituals, Religious and Secular, John W. Work. This authoritative study traces the African influences of songs sung and played by black Americans at work, in church, and as entertainment. The author discusses the lyric significance of such songs as "Swing Low, Sweet Chariot," "John Henry," and others and offers the words and music for 230 songs. Bibliography. Index of Song Titles. 272pp. 6½ x 9¼. 40271-1

MOVIE-STAR PORTRAITS OF THE FORTIES, John Kobal (ed.). 163 glamor, studio photos of 106 stars of the 1940s: Rita Hayworth, Ava Gardner, Marlon Brando, Clark Gable, many more. 176pp. 8⅜ x 11¼. 23546-7

BENCHLEY LOST AND FOUND, Robert Benchley. Finest humor from early 30s, about pet peeves, child psychologists, post office and others. Mostly unavailable elsewhere. 73 illustrations by Peter Arno and others. 183pp. 5⅜ x 8½. 22410-4

YEKL and THE IMPORTED BRIDEGROOM AND OTHER STORIES OF YIDDISH NEW YORK, Abraham Cahan. Film Hester Street based on *Yekl* (1896). Novel, other stories among first about Jewish immigrants on N.Y.'s East Side. 240pp. 5⅜ x 8½. 22427-9

SELECTED POEMS, Walt Whitman. Generous sampling from *Leaves of Grass*. Twenty-four poems include "I Hear America Singing," "Song of the Open Road," "I Sing the Body Electric," "When Lilacs Last in the Dooryard Bloom'd," "O Captain! My Captain!"–all reprinted from an authoritative edition. Lists of titles and first lines. 128pp. 5³⁄₁₆ x 8¼. 26878-0

MY BONDAGE AND MY FREEDOM, Frederick Douglass. Born a slave, Douglass became outspoken force in antislavery movement. The best of Douglass' autobiographies. Graphic description of slave life. 464pp. 5⅜ x 8½. 22457-0

FOLLOWING THE EQUATOR: A Journey Around the World, Mark Twain. Fascinating humorous account of 1897 voyage to Hawaii, Australia, India, New Zealand, etc. Ironic, bemused reports on peoples, customs, climate, flora and fauna, politics, much more. 197 illustrations. 720pp. 5⅜ x 8½. 26113-1

THE PEOPLE CALLED SHAKERS, Edward D. Andrews. Definitive study of Shakers: origins, beliefs, practices, dances, social organization, furniture and crafts, etc. 33 illustrations. 351pp. 5⅜ x 8½. 21081-2

THE MYTHS OF GREECE AND ROME, H. A. Guerber. A classic of mythology, generously illustrated, long prized for its simple, graphic, accurate retelling of the principal myths of Greece and Rome, and for its commentary on their origins and significance. With 64 illustrations by Michelangelo, Raphael, Titian, Rubens, Canova, Bernini and others. 480pp. 5⅜ x 8½. 27584-1

PSYCHOLOGY OF MUSIC, Carl E. Seashore. Classic work discusses music as a medium from psychological viewpoint. Clear treatment of physical acoustics, auditory apparatus, sound perception, development of musical skills, nature of musical feeling, host of other topics. 88 figures. 408pp. 5⅜ x 8½. 21851-1

THE PHILOSOPHY OF HISTORY, Georg W. Hegel. Great classic of Western thought develops concept that history is not chance but rational process, the evolution of freedom. 457pp. 5⅜ x 8½. 20112-0

THE BOOK OF TEA, Kakuzo Okakura. Minor classic of the Orient: entertaining, charming explanation, interpretation of traditional Japanese culture in terms of tea ceremony. 94pp. 5⅜ x 8½. 20070-1

LIFE IN ANCIENT EGYPT, Adolf Erman. Fullest, most thorough, detailed older account with much not in more recent books, domestic life, religion, magic, medicine, commerce, much more. Many illustrations reproduce tomb paintings, carvings, hieroglyphs, etc. 597pp. 5⅜ x 8½. 22632-8

SUNDIALS, Their Theory and Construction, Albert Waugh. Far and away the best, most thorough coverage of ideas, mathematics concerned, types, construction, adjusting anywhere. Simple, nontechnical treatment allows even children to build several of these dials. Over 100 illustrations. 230pp. 5⅜ x 8½. 22947-5

THEORETICAL HYDRODYNAMICS, L. M. Milne-Thomson. Classic exposition of the mathematical theory of fluid motion, applicable to both hydrodynamics and aerodynamics. Over 600 exercises. 768pp. 6⅛ x 9¼. 68970-0

SONGS OF EXPERIENCE: Facsimile Reproduction with 26 Plates in Full Color, William Blake. 26 full-color plates from a rare 1826 edition. Includes "The Tyger," "London," "Holy Thursday," and other poems. Printed text of poems. 48pp. 5¼ x 7. 24636-1

OLD-TIME VIGNETTES IN FULL COLOR, Carol Belanger Grafton (ed.). Over 390 charming, often sentimental illustrations, selected from archives of Victorian graphics—pretty women posing, children playing, food, flowers, kittens and puppies, smiling cherubs, birds and butterflies, much more. All copyright-free. 48pp. 9¼ x 12¼. 27269-9

PIANO TUNING, J. Cree Fischer. Clearest, best book for beginner, amateur. Simple repairs, raising dropped notes, tuning by easy method of flattened fifths. No previous skills needed. 4 illustrations. 201pp. 5⅜ x 8½. 23267-0

HINTS TO SINGERS, Lillian Nordica. Selecting the right teacher, developing confidence, overcoming stage fright, and many other important skills receive thoughtful discussion in this indispensible guide, written by a world-famous diva of four decades' experience. 96pp. 5⅜ x 8½. 40094-8

THE COMPLETE NONSENSE OF EDWARD LEAR, Edward Lear. All nonsense limericks, zany alphabets, Owl and Pussycat, songs, nonsense botany, etc., illustrated by Lear. Total of 320pp. 5⅜ x 8½. (Available in U.S. only.) 20167-8

VICTORIAN PARLOUR POETRY: An Annotated Anthology, Michael R. Turner. 117 gems by Longfellow, Tennyson, Browning, many lesser-known poets. "The Village Blacksmith," "Curfew Must Not Ring Tonight," "Only a Baby Small," dozens more, often difficult to find elsewhere. Index of poets, titles, first lines. xxiii + 325pp. 5⅜ x 8¼. 27044-0

DUBLINERS, James Joyce. Fifteen stories offer vivid, tightly focused observations of the lives of Dublin's poorer classes. At least one, "The Dead," is considered a masterpiece. Reprinted complete and unabridged from standard edition. 160pp. 5³⁄₁₆ x 8¼. 26870-5

GREAT WEIRD TALES: 14 Stories by Lovecraft, Blackwood, Machen and Others, S. T. Joshi (ed.). 14 spellbinding tales, including "The Sin Eater," by Fiona McLeod, "The Eye Above the Mantel," by Frank Belknap Long, as well as renowned works by R. H. Barlow, Lord Dunsany, Arthur Machen, W. C. Morrow and eight other masters of the genre. 256pp. 5⅜ x 8½. (Available in U.S. only.) 40436-6

THE BOOK OF THE SACRED MAGIC OF ABRAMELIN THE MAGE, translated by S. MacGregor Mathers. Medieval manuscript of ceremonial magic. Basic document in Aleister Crowley, Golden Dawn groups. 268pp. 5⅜ x 8½. 23211-5

NEW RUSSIAN-ENGLISH AND ENGLISH-RUSSIAN DICTIONARY, M. A. O'Brien. This is a remarkably handy Russian dictionary, containing a surprising amount of information, including over 70,000 entries. 366pp. 4½ x 6⅛. 20208-9

HISTORIC HOMES OF THE AMERICAN PRESIDENTS, Second, Revised Edition, Irvin Haas. A traveler's guide to American Presidential homes, most open to the public, depicting and describing homes occupied by every American President from George Washington to George Bush. With visiting hours, admission charges, travel routes. 175 photographs. Index. 160pp. 8¼ x 11. 26751-2

NEW YORK IN THE FORTIES, Andreas Feininger. 162 brilliant photographs by the well-known photographer, formerly with *Life* magazine. Commuters, shoppers, Times Square at night, much else from city at its peak. Captions by John von Hartz. 181pp. 9¼ x 10¾. 23585-8

INDIAN SIGN LANGUAGE, William Tomkins. Over 525 signs developed by Sioux and other tribes. Written instructions and diagrams. Also 290 pictographs. 111pp. 6⅛ x 9¼. 22029-X

PHOTOGRAPHIC SKETCHBOOK OF THE CIVIL WAR, Alexander Gardner. 100 photos taken on field during the Civil War. Famous shots of Manassas Harper's Ferry, Lincoln, Richmond, slave pens, etc. 244pp. 10⅝ x 8¼. 22731-6

FIVE ACRES AND INDEPENDENCE, Maurice G. Kains. Great back-to-the-land classic explains basics of self-sufficient farming. The one book to get. 95 illustrations. 397pp. 5⅜ x 8½. 20974-1

SONGS OF EASTERN BIRDS, Dr. Donald J. Borror. Songs and calls of 60 species most common to eastern U.S.: warblers, woodpeckers, flycatchers, thrushes, larks, many more in high-quality recording. Cassette and manual 99912-2

A MODERN HERBAL, Margaret Grieve. Much the fullest, most exact, most useful compilation of herbal material. Gigantic alphabetical encyclopedia, from aconite to zedoary, gives botanical information, medical properties, folklore, economic uses, much else. Indispensable to serious reader. 161 illustrations. 888pp. 6½ x 9¼. 2-vol. set. (Available in U.S. only.) Vol. I: 22798-7
Vol. II: 22799-5

HIDDEN TREASURE MAZE BOOK, Dave Phillips. Solve 34 challenging mazes accompanied by heroic tales of adventure. Evil dragons, people-eating plants, blood-thirsty giants, many more dangerous adversaries lurk at every twist and turn. 34 mazes, stories, solutions. 48pp. 8¼ x 11. 24566-7

LETTERS OF W. A. MOZART, Wolfgang A. Mozart. Remarkable letters show bawdy wit, humor, imagination, musical insights, contemporary musical world; includes some letters from Leopold Mozart. 276pp. 5⅜ x 8½. 22859-2

BASIC PRINCIPLES OF CLASSICAL BALLET, Agrippina Vaganova. Great Russian theoretician, teacher explains methods for teaching classical ballet. 118 illustrations. 175pp. 5⅜ x 8½. 22036-2

THE JUMPING FROG, Mark Twain. Revenge edition. The original story of The Celebrated Jumping Frog of Calaveras County, a hapless French translation, and Twain's hilarious "retranslation" from the French. 12 illustrations. 66pp. 5⅜ x 8½. 22686-7

BEST REMEMBERED POEMS, Martin Gardner (ed.). The 126 poems in this superb collection of 19th- and 20th-century British and American verse range from Shelley's "To a Skylark" to the impassioned "Renascence" of Edna St. Vincent Millay and to Edward Lear's whimsical "The Owl and the Pussycat." 224pp. 5⅜ x 8½. 27165-X

COMPLETE SONNETS, William Shakespeare. Over 150 exquisite poems deal with love, friendship, the tyranny of time, beauty's evanescence, death and other themes in language of remarkable power, precision and beauty. Glossary of archaic terms. 80pp. 5$\frac{3}{16}$ x 8¼. 26686-9

THE BATTLES THAT CHANGED HISTORY, Fletcher Pratt. Eminent historian profiles 16 crucial conflicts, ancient to modern, that changed the course of civilization. 352pp. 5⅜ x 8½. 41129-X

THE STORY OF THE TITANIC AS TOLD BY ITS SURVIVORS, Jack Winocour (ed.). What it was really like. Panic, despair, shocking inefficiency, and a little heroism. More thrilling than any fictional account. 26 illustrations. 320pp. 5⅜ x 8½. 20610-6

FAIRY AND FOLK TALES OF THE IRISH PEASANTRY, William Butler Yeats (ed.). Treasury of 64 tales from the twilight world of Celtic myth and legend: "The Soul Cages," "The Kildare Pooka," "King O'Toole and his Goose," many more. Introduction and Notes by W. B. Yeats. 352pp. 5⅜ x 8½. 26941-8

BUDDHIST MAHAYANA TEXTS, E. B. Cowell and others (eds.). Superb, accurate translations of basic documents in Mahayana Buddhism, highly important in history of religions. The Buddha-karita of Asvaghosha, Larger Sukhavativyuha, more. 448pp. 5⅜ x 8½. 25552-2

ONE TWO THREE . . . INFINITY: Facts and Speculations of Science, George Gamow. Great physicist's fascinating, readable overview of contemporary science: number theory, relativity, fourth dimension, entropy, genes, atomic structure, much more. 128 illustrations. Index. 352pp. 5⅜ x 8½. 25664-2

EXPERIMENTATION AND MEASUREMENT, W. J. Youden. Introductory manual explains laws of measurement in simple terms and offers tips for achieving accuracy and minimizing errors. Mathematics of measurement, use of instruments, experimenting with machines. 1994 edition. Foreword. Preface. Introduction. Epilogue. Selected Readings. Glossary. Index. Tables and figures. 128pp. 5⅜ x 8½. 40451-X

DALÍ ON MODERN ART: The Cuckolds of Antiquated Modern Art, Salvador Dalí. Influential painter skewers modern art and its practitioners. Outrageous evaluations of Picasso, Cézanne, Turner, more. 15 renderings of paintings discussed. 44 calligraphic decorations by Dalí. 96pp. 5⅜ x 8½. (Available in U.S. only.) 29220-7

ANTIQUE PLAYING CARDS: A Pictorial History, Henry René D'Allemagne. Over 900 elaborate, decorative images from rare playing cards (14th–20th centuries): Bacchus, death, dancing dogs, hunting scenes, royal coats of arms, players cheating, much more. 96pp. 9¼ x 12¼. 29265-7

MAKING FURNITURE MASTERPIECES: 30 Projects with Measured Drawings, Franklin H. Gottshall. Step-by-step instructions, illustrations for constructing handsome, useful pieces, among them a Sheraton desk, Chippendale chair, Spanish desk, Queen Anne table and a William and Mary dressing mirror. 224pp. 8⅛ x 11¼. 29338-6

THE FOSSIL BOOK: A Record of Prehistoric Life, Patricia V. Rich et al. Profusely illustrated definitive guide covers everything from single-celled organisms and dinosaurs to birds and mammals and the interplay between climate and man. Over 1,500 illustrations. 760pp. 7½ x 10⅛. 29371-8

Paperbound unless otherwise indicated. Available at your book dealer, online at **www.doverpublications.com**, or by writing to Dept. GI, Dover Publications, Inc., 31 East 2nd Street, Mineola, NY 11501. For current price information or for free catalogues (please indicate field of interest), write to Dover Publications or log on to **www.doverpublications.com** and see every Dover book in print. Dover publishes more than 500 books each year on science, elementary and advanced mathematics, biology, music, art, literary history, social sciences, and other areas.